Your Name & Colors

Secret Keys to Your Beauty, Personality & Success!

THE ROLLIET
LETTER-COLOR THEORY
BY D. G. ROLLIET

About the Author

D.G. Rolliet has been involved in the fashion and color fields for over 16 years. He has designed and analyzed garments and colors for major department stores, exclusive boutiques, major corporations, and many individuals in the entertainment field. He has spoken at numerous educational institutions and is continuing his studies of the effects of colors in relation to human character traits.

For further information regarding individual, home or business color consultations, phone Mr. Rolliet at (415) 787-1810 or write to: Color Diplomats, P.O. Box 21, Crockett, CA 94525

Your Name and Colors
Secret Keys to Your
Beauty, Personality & Success

The Rolliet Letter-Color Theory

Author: D.G. Rolliet
Publisher: Spectra Publishing House, P.O. Box 21, Crockett, CA 94525
ISBN Number 0-9621693-0-7
Library of Congress catalog number 89-091991

Printed in Korea

Cover design and color concept by D.G. Rolliet
Cover illustration by Ed Sherwood, Illustrius
Photography by Barry Evans Studio, Barry Evans and Jamie Hardin
Graphic Production by Janet Tumpich
Makeup by Christine Carpenter.

Special thanks to Michael Renault and Jeanne Wolfe for editing; and models – Augie Pecorelli, Bill Doty, Carolyn Anderson, Heidi Bickham, Irene Hald, Margaret Johnson, Sheila Furbush, and to Michael and Diana Adams for their help in making this book possible.

Preface

I would like to clarify from the start that the following
formulas and philosophies in this book are not intended
as any new religion or in any way intended to replace religious teachings. God has given us many tools to discover,
that can be used to enrich our daily lives if we use them in
moderation. I hope this book will be one of those tools
that can help to enrich those that use it, and use it in
moderation – not as a solve-all source. I hope you enjoy
it, and I wish you success in all good things that you try
to accomplish.

D.G. Rolliet

Contents

Introduction

This book was written to share my discoveries of how amazingly accurate a person's name, and the letters in a person's name as well as their sequence, which determine the basic foundations of a person's life-long character-chemistries and talents, of the following energy centers: spiritual, mental, vocal, physical, control, emotional, and sexual.

This book will examine how the colors that are attuned to each letter of a person's name, determines these personal character traits, which we can use in helping to determine our careers, money making abilities, talents, home decor environment, love mates, wardrobe colors, etc. They basically determine why we think, speak, feel, project, etc. in the ways we do.

The Rolliet Letter-Color Theory can be used to:

1. Uplift one's spirit - (spiritual center) tune into the youthful color and traits, and project youthfulness, cleanliness, wholesomeness, and creativeness.

2. Increase ones intellectual capabilities - (mental center) and tune into the intellectual color and traits; and be more analytical and intellectual.

3. Tune into one's vocal expressions - (vocal center) and tune into one's vocal color and traits; and increase one's fluency and vocabulary.

4. Stimulate and capitalize on one's physical talents - (physical center) and physical color and traits and become more dramatic and physical.

5. Cultivate self-control and sense of power - (control center) and tune into the regal color and traits and appear more in control and refined.

6. Relax one's emotions - (emotional center) and tune into one's feminine color and traits; and project relaxed and romantic.

7. Enhance and enjoy one's sexual life - (sexual center) and tune into one's sexual color and traits; and project seductiveness, sexuality, and sensuality.

8. Tune into color auras in any of these centers to enhance your beauty and preferred visual image.

9. Learn how to understand and communicate with love-mates, friends, relatives and others.

I foresee, in the near future, that the formulas that I explain in this book will be used not only by a vast amount of individuals but also by the following:

- Advertisement Industry
- Art Directors
- Artists
- Career Consultants
- Entertainment Industry
- Fashion and Jewelry Industries
- Historians
- Hospitals, Doctors, Mental Health Counselors
- Image Consultants, Photographers
- Interior Decorators, Paint and Home Furnishings Companies
- Educational Institutions
- Mail Order Industries
- Major Corporations
- Marriage Consultants, Dating Services
- Modeling Agencies
- Music Teachers and Musicians
- Parents (in choosing infant's names and raising children)
- Scientists
- Sex Therapists
- Small Businesses
- Spiritualists

• Sports Organizations/Athletes

• Wardrobe, Make-up, and Color Consultants

. . . and many more.

I hope this book will bring physical scientists to work closer with the spiritual scientists using spiritual teachings which were divinely intended as a guide, to help us to live more harmoniously with each other.

I would like to thank God, Ann Shaw, Roland T. Hunt, Corinne Heline, Faber Birren, Sir Isaac Newton, my family, friends and all those that have contributed to this book. Many thanks to the numerous people that I've interviewed through the years, and especially to women who have continually complimented my findings and have consistently given me the extra incentive and confidence to write this book. I would like to share some of those compliments which I received:

What else is in your Crystal Ball?

That's amazing!

That's exactly me.

That's so accurate, it's scary!

That's incredible!

I've never thought of it in that way before!

That makes sense, alot of sense!

How did you know that?

How did you learn all this ?

That's outstanding, remarkable!

Would you please teach me.

You know me better than I know myself!

That's very interesting - ... very interesting.

Thank you, all of you; the book you've waited so eagerly for is finally available!

I would like to challenge anyone who doubts my findings. Research and test these findings for yourself, I feel confident that your findings will support my findings to a large degree.

Spiritual and scientific color studies have been going on for many years and just like any other new or unproven field, skepticism will be prevalent. Spiritual and scientific color philosophies have been denounced by many, but it is my belief and others that it is making a very strong comeback due to new discoveries, new technologies, and increased awareness in general, all of which will give this field higher recognition. I hope this book will contribute to this aim. All theories, inventions, discoveries, and philosophies must go through a trial and error period. Relatively unexplored ideas endure a period of hard times, until proven and accepted. Some are already proven, such as, spiritual persons have claimed that humans and all living beings emit an aura, which has now been proven with new technologies (an electroencephalograph (EEG), Kirlian photography, etc.). Many top scientific organizations, businesses, and governments have or are studying the spiritual, physical, and emotional effects of color. Some of the organizations that have been involved or published information regarding one or more of these effects of colors are listed as follows:

• American Academy of Ophthalmology and Otolaryngology
• American Journal of Psychology
• American Society for Photobiology
• Canadian Medical Association Journal
• Foundation of Optometry
• Illuminating Engineering Society
• Inter-Society Color Council
• Japanese Journal of Obstetrics And Gynecology
• Journal of Experimental Psychology
• National Bureau of Standards
• National Library Press

- National Research Bureau, Inc.
- National Society for the Prevention of Blindness
- New York Zoological Society
- Ohio State University
- Oxford University Press
- Pittsburg Plate Glass Company of Tampa Florida
- Public Buildings Administration
- Smithsonian Institute
- U.S. Army
- U.S. Navy
- U.S. Public Health Service, Washington D.C.
- U.S. State Department
- U.S. Veterans Hospital, Oakland, CA
- Yoga Publications Society;

. . . and many more.

I foresee in the near future when highly sensitive electromagnetic visual and audio equipment (some of which are being tested today) will be able to tune into a person's vibrational tone and color rate in any of their seven energy centers and help in uplifting one's spirit, especially for those that are depressed. Increase and clear one's mental center, help in tuning into one's vocal vibrations for singers and other vocal applications, for stimulating one's physical body for exercise and other purposes; for stimulating one's control center to curb or cure addictive and compulsive problems and phobias. To relax one's emotional center to relieve emotional problems; to tune into ones sexual center for stimulation or sexual dysfunction.

Employers will use some of these services to increase worker productivity, resulting in millions of dollars saved from time lost by employees suffering from problems such as stress disorders and other problems, which are on the rise. I also foresee a day when homes will have these same services built right in as standard equipment. Doctors and hospitals will use them on a daily basis. There is already light and audio machines that are being used to reset a person's biological clock from effects of jet lag and for transmitting subliminal messages to increase intellect, memory, and other brain functions. The possible applications of these services are mind boggling!

I also feel this book will give greater insight into why we have different likes and dislikes such as: you might think someone is physically or sexually attractive whereas your best friend may think the opposite; you might like classical music, but others don't; or you might like to go to the mountains to relax, but your partner likes to go sailing.

It will also answer why some individuals are natural singers and why others can't hardly sing a note; why some are very imaginative and creative while others lack these talents; and why some are great money makers and some not!

1
The Seven Centers

Seven Energy Centers

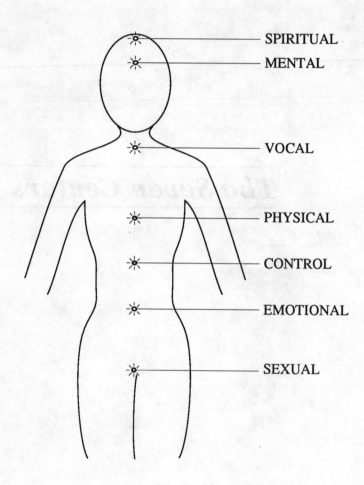

- SPIRITUAL
- MENTAL
- VOCAL
- PHYSICAL
- CONTROL
- EMOTIONAL
- SEXUAL

1

The Seven Centers

Upon awakening everyday most people will not ask themselves, "how do I feel spiritually today?" or "how do I feel?" or "where am I, mentally, vocally, physically, self-control, emotionally, and sexually?" We tend to generalize with general statements to express how we feel, such as, "I feel great," or "I feel lousy," or "I feel so-so," or "I feel ok." In making one of these statements, we are expressing either positive or negative feelings based on one of our seven centers; usually the most dominant one at that time. For example:

I feel great today. (All centers)

I have faith things will work out. (Spiritual and Control)

I'm depressed (Spiritual)

I feel youthful. (Spiritual)

I feel old. (Spiritual)

I feel sharp today. (Mental)

I'm confused. (Mental)

I can't seem to figure it out today. (Mental and Control)

I sound raspy today. (Vocal)

I feel sultry today. (Sexual)

I don't really care. (Sexual)

Loosen up! Let your hair down a little. (Sexual)

We can all recall situations when we have had conflicts between these different centers; for example,

times when our "control" center is tempted to blow up at someone but our practical intellectual mental center says "no don't do it!";

when we're tempted to get involved with someone emotionally or sexually but our mental or spiritual center says "no!";

when we're not feeling well physically whether from injury or illness, but our spiritual or emotional center says, "but I want to go and do things."

Most psychoanalysts or doctors in western cultures use three general categories to define these centers: physical, mental and emotional, or in other words, mind, body and soul.

Eastern cultures generally recognize seven centers and call them chakras.

2
The Seven Centers and the Senses

2

The Seven Centers and the Senses

Before I get directly into my findings I would first like to give examples of how our five senses can affect us through our seven energy centers as illustrated on page 8.

The Sense of Smell – When we smell:

1. Perfume: It stimulates the sexual center (just look at all media advertisements, almost all have a sexual message on some level!)

2. A rotten or poisonous odor:
   A. Spiritual - It is depressing.
   B. Mental - It causes fear and confusion.
   C. Physical - It causes muscle contraction and lung irritation.
   D. Emotional - It's upsetting.

3. Warm freshly laundered clothes:
   A. Spiritual - Wholesomeness, morality, and cleanliness
   B. Physical - Comfort, pleasure, softness, in touching
   C. Emotional - Security and calming

4. Good food:
   A. Spiritual - Uplifting, and rejuvenating
   B. Mental - Sense of confidence, good health; memory associations of places, people, and tastes.
   C. Emotional - Security, pleasing and calming

The Sense of Sight – What happens when you see?

1. Your lost dog or cat:
   A. Spiritual - Uplifting and cheerful
   B. Mental - Relief at the end of mental confusion
   C. Vocal - Talking and calling of the lost animal's name
   D. Physical - Stimulating by petting and hugging of the animal and clapping the hands
   E. Emotional - Relaxing and pleasing

2. Your team scores a touchdown:
   A. Spiritual - Uplifting and cheerful
   B Mental - Relief
   C. Vocal - Yelling and cheering
   D. Physical - Stimulating by jumping up and down and the clapping of hands
   E. Control - Confidence, reassuring and in control
   F. Emotional - Relaxing and pleasing

3. A dangerous object hurled at you:
   A. Spiritual - Depressing
   B. Mental - Fear of danger, confusion and memory - pain association
   C. Vocal - Yell or scream
   D. Physical - Muscle contraction and defensive reaction
   E. Control - Out of control, threat and panic
   F. Emotional - Upsetting

4. An attractive body with tight fitting pants, low neckline, slit skirt, etc.:
   A. Mental - Association with healthy body
   B. Control - Control is tested by temptation and patience
   C. Sexual - Stimulation and arousal

5. An attractive face:
   A. Mental - Self-image (your own appearance or organization)
   B. Physical - Grooming (combing of hair and straightening of clothes)
   C. Emotional - Romantic and pleasing

6. When you see someone or something suffering:
   A. Spiritual - Depression, compassion, empathy
   B. Physical - Touching and a need to comfort
   C. Control - Tested
   D. Emotional - Upsetting

7. A bright sunny day after several days of rain or fog:
   A. Spiritual - Uplifting and cheerful
   B. Mental - Confidence, clarity, and clearing
   C. Physical - Stimulating
   D. Control - Back in control (regaining control)
   E. Emotional - Relief and calming

8. Someone with a new luxury car or home when you can't afford one:
   A. Spiritual - Depressing
   B. Control - Patience tested and out of control
   C. Emotional - Upsetting

The Sense of Touch – What happens when you touch?

1. Something very hot:
   A. Spiritual - Depressing
   B. Mental - Danger, escape, worry, and confusion
   C. Physical - Pain in the nerve endings and muscle contraction
   D. Control - Out of Control
   E. Emotional - Upsetting

2. Something round and soft or smooth and silky:
   A. Mental - Pleasing
   B. Control - In control
   C. Emotional - Relaxing, comforting
   D. Sexual - Stimulation and excitement

3. Warm and freshly laundered clean clothes:
   A. Spiritual - Wholesomeness, cleanliness, and uplifting
   B. Mental - Confidence, healthy association
   C. Physical - Pleasure and comfort
   D. Emotional - Relaxing and security

Sense of Taste – What happens when you taste?

1. Good food:
   A. Spiritual - Uplifting and cheerful
   B. Mental - Confidence and sense of health
   C. Emotional - Comforting, relaxing, and security

2. Rotten or poisonous foods:
   A. Spiritual - Depressing
   B. Mental - Worry, fear, and confusion
   C. Physical - Cramps, bitterness, and muscle contractions
   D. Emotional - Upsetting

3. Certain ethnic or holiday foods:
   A. Spiritual - Wholesomeness and uplifting
   B. Mental - Memory stimulation of family members and cultural associations
   C. Emotional - Security

The Sense of Hearing – What happens when you hear?

This is the "sense" that we are the most concerned with because letters and colors vibrate in electromagnetic wavelengths which enter our ears enroute to our brains (which I will explain later in this chapter).

1. Someone yell real loud, "Watch out!":
   A. Spiritual - Depressing
   B. Mental - Fear and confusion
   C. Control - Loss of control
   D. Emotional - Upsetting

2. Someone in a nice sweet voice saying Hi! How are you today?
   A. Spiritual - Uplifting and wholesome
   B. Mental - Confidence (positive)
   C. Control - In control and poised
   D. Emotional - Pleasing and relaxing

3. Someone saying to you - "You sure look tired (sickly, or unhealthy) today!":
   A. Spiritual - Depressing
   B. Mental - Worry, fear, and stress
   C. Control - Loss of control
   D. Emotional - Upsetting

4. Someone saying to you - "You sure look nice today!":
   A. Spiritual - Uplifting and cheerful
   B. Mental - Confidence
   C. Control - In control, poised
   D. Emotional - Pleasing and relaxing

5. Music you like
   A. Spiritual - Uplifting and cheerful
   B. Vocal - Start to sing along
   C. Physical - Movement, dancing, clapping, tapping
   D. Emotional - Relaxing

Now we have established that our different senses can stimulate in either positive or negative ways our seven energy centers and that these seven centers do exist.

I would now like to explain how our senses can affect our seven centers in an immediate and dramatic way and in slow subtle ways, but also how the slow subtle ways can have a strong influence over an extended period of time. As examples:

When you smell: A slightly unpleasant odor, your reaction will be slow and subtle.

When you smell: Ammonia or a strong chemical or poison, your reaction will be immediate and dramatic.

When you see: Someone walking at you slowly with a shopping cart in a store, your reaction to get out of the way will be slow and subtle.

When you see: A dangerous object pointed or hurled at you, your reaction will be immediate and dramatic.

When you touch: A object that's a little warm, your reaction will be slow and subtle.

When you touch: A very hot object, your reaction will be immediate and dramatic.

When you taste: Food that's slightly salty, your reaction will be slow and subtle.

When you taste: Food that's very bitter, your reaction will be immediate and dramatic.

When you hear: Someone call your name, your reaction will be slow and subtle.

When you hear: A very loud explosion, your reaction will be immediate and dramatic.

Now that we see how we're conditioned to react in appropriate ways depending on the situation, let me give you a few examples of how subtle experiences can have very dramatic and profound affects on us.

What if (and I advise against anyone to trying this example, I only use it as an example to prove a point) someone were to pinch the back of your arm in a mild manner, but continued for a few thousand times. Your arm would become extremely sore and swollen and you would become very irritated, right? This is the way in which torture is usually administered in a slow, continuous manner. Now, after being pinched on the back of your arm repeatedly over a long period of time, if you were given the option of being pinched one time real hard or pinched gently another few thousand times, we would all probably say "Just one more time," and "Get it over with quickly!" instead of enduring the long lasting pain over a long period of time!

What happens to a person who worries over a period of many years - the result can be a nervous breakdown. What can happen to a person who consumes a *bad diet* over a period of many years - they will probably de- velop a very serious physical health condition. What about when someone has been depressed for a long period of time, dramatic effects can manifest in an emotional or mental breakdown.

So now we see that not only does the amount of times, but also the passage of time affects us at first in subtle ways, but then can lead to very dramatic results. This is the same manner as how your name called to you over and over thousands of times affects you from infancy through adulthood by way of the sense of hearing, which leads to your brain, which effects your spiritual energy centers, by way of different color trait wavelengths and vibrations. Roland T. Hunt in his book "The Eighth Key to Color" put it like this: "Man has seven sensory-motor association areas in the brain (five only in textbooks of modern medical science). These are the brain areas of registration where the senses are coordinated with the functional organs of the body, under the control of the thalamus. Each of these response areas is attuned to a different color in the spectrum and each has it's own record of experience with thalamic Indigo on the threshold and overall keeper of the archives." This is precisely where my discoveries start. And those discoveries are how the letters and their sequence in your name, and the characteristics of the colors that are attuned to those letters, and how they effect our seven centers in building our general character traits (our life-long color traits). I have also discovered seven basic formulas or methods of finding a person's daily colors, and traits, or character moods.

In a study done at a major university in California, forty-eight patients were told while unconscious during surgery, to touch their ear. Thirty-three out of the forty-eight actually touched their ear. Proving that the mind and its interconnecting body parts, even while unconscious, reacts from the sense of hearing. The reaction in this case happened to be a physical one.

"The skin's electrical activity changed remarkably when ears heard words associated with emotion." – *Carl Jung*

Let me try to clear up any doubt or confusion about colors entering a person's ear by way of the letter sounds of our names. As I stated earlier sounds vibrate color auras. The reason why the normal human eye cannot see those color auras from these letter sounds is because they are very subtle and very short in length and impulse. Colors that we can see vibrate at 1/33 per second or 1/33,000 of an inch at the red end of the spectrum, and 1/67 per second or 1/67,000 of an inch at the violet end. Any color impulses below these are invisible. It is my belief that the letter-sounds that we hear from our names therefore carry with them either invisible subtle color auras which enter our ears en route to our brain, or the other possibility is, the letter vibrations in our names activate their corresponding colors in our inner ear cochlea fluid (just as moisture in the air after it rains acts as a prism and produces a rainbow), which sends the color vibration to our brain, which in turn sends this color-coded message to its corresponding center. Remember the earlier examples of explaining how subtle forces eventually have strong influences upon us. Since our birth, we have heard our name repeated thousands of times, and the traits of the colors that vibrate to those names have affected our seven energy centers and helped to lay the basic foundations of these centers.

Some will ask, "how can an invisible color vibration have a spiritual character trait," and probably follow with "that's poppycock" or "that's a bunch of hocus-pocus." However, almost all spiritual occurrences or miracles throughout history have been mysterious and physically or scientifically unexplainable. Apparently this is God's plan. Jesus stated the way to the spiritual heaven was by way of our "faith" and "belief" in His dying for us. If one is to believe this book, then one will probably need a certain amount of faith in subjects of a spiritual nature. But just as God gives us proof of His truth when we live by His teachings and reap the gifts and rewards for our belief in His teachings, I shall try to prove the truth of the formulas in this book by citing name examples and permit the reader to judge, by way of one's memory recall of one's life-long character traits and daily traits by asking, "are these the ways I've projected spiritually, mentally, emotionally, etc.?" I've also included color photos to help in proving some of the formulas of this book.

I conclude this chapter by asking these questions to those that will only accept physical proof of a scientific nature. If a medical team were to dissect a human body, would any of them be able to show us that person's spirit, emotions, or mental thoughts? No, they wouldn't. They could only show us bits and pieces of flesh, muscles, nerves, blood, fat, etc., all physical substances. Yet we all are witnesses that a human being possesses these different feelings of spirit, mental thoughts, emotions (happiness, sadness, romance) and all the other feelings that we have experienced. Yet a team of medical doctors could not lay any of these feelings out on a table and say, "here they are." Therefore, they are physically invisible, right? If what I've just reasoned holds true, then it shouldn't be hard to believe the philosophies outlined in this book.

"Science can only be created by those thoroughly imbued with the aspiration toward truth and understanding. This source of feeling, however, springs from the sphere of religion, science without religion is lame, religion without science is blind." –Albert Einstein

3
The Letter-Color Code

3
The Letter-Color Code

In the late 17th century Sir Isaac Newton announced his discovery of how sunlight (white light) could be separated into the seven colors of the spectrum by way of the prism. This is fairly well known, but Newton also aligned (attuned) the seven colors to the Diatonic Scale (the musical scale): red to C, orange to D, yellow to E, green to F, blue to G, indigo (flesh) to A, violet to B. The reason I've substituted "Flesh" for indigo because it is my belief and to my knowledge that in Newton's day the deep-blue-violet dye from the indigo plant was frequently mixed with certain chemicals and acids in their research which produced a copper-flesh color (similar to the color of a person's skin when they get a coppery suntan). This color was also known by the names of brown indigo and copper indigo, so this is the color that I believe Newton was referring to when he used the name indigo and not the deep-blue-violet. Other names used to describe the flesh colors are Tan, Beige and Brown and Earth Colors depending on the tint or shade. This will be discussed later in the flesh color chapter.

All things that are alive, vibrate a wavelength and an aura. Humans, animals, plants, insects, and sounds. Here is the color alphabet that aligns (attunes) all of the wavelength vibrations of the letters of the alphabet to the seven colors.

Flesh	Violet	Red	Orange	Yellow	Green	Blue
A	B	C	D	E	F	G
H	I	J	K	L	M	N
O	P	Q	R	S	T	U
V	W	X	Y	Z		

4
Your Name

4
Your Name

Before you align the letters in your name to their colors and their characteristics, you must first establish your real name and the actual sound (pronunciation of your name). When I say your real name, I mean the name in which you were called the most during your lifetime. If you had a nickname that you were called by your relatives and friends much more frequently than your official given name, then you would use that nickname to analyze your colors. If in the case, you were called a nickname and your official given name both on a regular basis, you will have the colors of both. If you have been called by your official name most of your life, then you will analyze from that name. Also take into consideration for example, that when a person drops a letter or letters (such as "Bobby" to "Bob" or "Robert" when they get older or "Sandy" and then later to "Sandra" etc.). When a person changes a name one will have character changes - but at times one will fall back into or retain, to a small degree, one's earlier characteristics.

One of the first actions that a movie company takes when it discovers a new budding star or starlet - is to change that person's name to create a certain image that they want this person to project. In the example again of a young man called "Bobby," they may just change it to "Bob" or "Robert" to give the name a more masculine sound. The higher sounding letters (especially the higher sounding "E") will project a more youthful, spirited, or more feminine characteristics, whereas the lower sounding letters will project a serious more earthier, or masculine image.

In establishing your real name, use the actual sound (pronunciation) of your name. For example, in the name "Cathy." the "C" is not pronounced as a"C" but as a "K" so a person would analyze it as a "K," and align it to the orange spectrum color characteristics. Also the "Y" on the end actually sounds to "E," so this person would use "E," which is a yellow letter. Jesus actually sounds like "Gee-zas" or if used in the Latin speaking people it would sound to "Ha-zuss or Julio would sound "Hu-lee-o". Use the letters that sound to these rather than the way they're spelled. You must also consider silent letters, if a letter is silent in the pronunciation of your name, don't use it. If it doesn't sound then it doesn't apply. For example,"Eileen," the "E" is silent, so this person's first letter analyzing will be analyzed as a "I" pronounced "I-leen." In a lot of names C's will sound to an S sound and in other names J's will sound to G's – in some cases it will be hard to determine which letters they sound to. If this happens to be the case in your name, just go to the different color chapters in this book to help you determine what color traits better fit your personality in the center that there is a question to what color a particular letter sounds to.

Also, consider the speed in which a name is pronounced. For example, the name "Dennis," if you were to say this name real slow it would sound to "Den-nas". But in reality the normal speed at which the name Dennis is pronounced is "Den-as," or at a faster speed it is "Den-s." Remember, analyze as close as possible to the sound of your name!

I've often been asked in both earnest and in sarcastic tones the question: "Well what if two people have the same name; does that mean they're going to be exactly alike?" I've also been asked, "Well, how can my name affect me when I had no choice of what my name would be?" In answer to the first question, a very firm No! I feel the odds against two people being exactly alike are extremely high because of two logical reasons. The first reason is the fact that our lives are influenced by many factors such as the environmental influences of where we were born. Also, history shows us how different generations are subject to time period beliefs and customs. We call these social and peer influences. For example, someone who was born and raised in a large city such as Los Angeles will differ dramatically from someone who was born in a swamp land community of Louisiana. Each individual is also influenced by their parents, how they treat us and influence us, what their beliefs and habits are, as well as their social and financial status. Also, during a lifetime two people will not come in contact or befriend the same set of friends or associates, whose beliefs can influence an individual's make-up. There are also biological differences. One person may be shorter or taller, overweight or thin, attractive or plain. Did we have any choice to any of these matters? So, it would be extremely unlikely for two people with the same name to be exactly alike.

But that is not all. We also have the "God-given" gift of free will to make our own decisions and to cultivate whatever character traits we wish. Some decide to choose good traits, others bad. Some decide to be compassionate, but others not. Some decide to be spiritual, others not. Some decide to cultivate their creative talents, others cultivate their destructive side. Some decide to cultivate their physical abilities, others their mental abilities. Just as what type of home gets built on top of its foundation depends on several factors (based on social, geographical, and personal preferences), we also have free will preference to build or cultivate whatever traits we choose (good or bad) off of our foundation.

In the following chapters, just as a scientist proves his hypothesis by repeated testing, I will try to prove my findings by the numerous name examples that I use.

5
Your Letters
and Their Centers

5
Your Letters and Their Centers

Here are my discoveries through my observations and research on these letter-colors in a person's name and how they affect or stimulate a person's general life-long moods and characteristics in one's seven energy centers. I also refer to these colors as life-long colors. Your life-long colors should be used in long-term uses such as decorating your home, relating to love mates, careers, and natural talents. Later in this book I will explain about our daily colors which affect our daily moods and not our general life-long character attributes. (Using the letter-color chart on page 22 align your following centers to their corresponding colors.)

After you have completed reading about each of your centers and center colors, turn to the *Do It Yourself Color Chart* page at the back of the book and list your life-long center colors, traits, and talents for reference and use in Wardrobe, Home-Decor, and Career possibilities.

Note: I would also advise reading chapters eleven through fifteen before finalizing your chart.

Spiritual Center
Top and Middle of Head

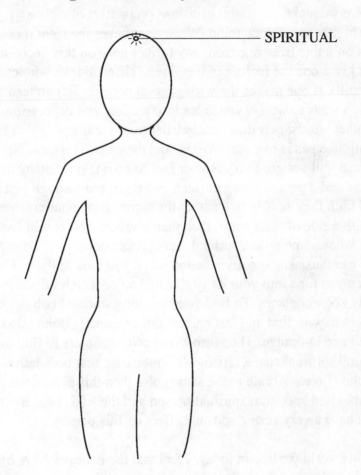

—————— SPIRITUAL

Your Spiritual Center Letters and Colors

The characteristics of the colors that are attuned to the first letters in your first and last name stimulate your spiritual center which is located at the crown of your head (as illustrated on page 29). Our spiritual center is where we make our moral decisions on matters of right and wrong. It is our higher conscience mind. When one makes the right moral decision and acts on it this frees one from any further guilt on this decision. Therefore, this gives one the feeling of happiness, cheerfulness, wholesomeness (free of guilt). If one makes the wrong moral decision, it can lead to guilt, which leads to worry, which leads to anxiety and depression. One's spirit, in other words, gets downgraded, depressed and low. Spirit is to a human being like gas is to a car. No gas, and the car will not go. No spirit, and the human will not go. Spirit is your fuel to go on. How many times have you witnessed a person going through bad times but through just sheer spirit and faith they're able to weather the storm. If one has cultivated the positive side of their spirit, then their spiritual colors will look youthful and wholesome on and around them. These colors will have a very sparkling enthusiastic quality reaction when you look at them. Especially when you tune into your daily spiritual color which I discuss later in the daily color chapters. To find your life-long spiritual colors use the first letters in your first and last names. For example, (J)ohn (D)oe vibrates to J-red and D-orange. Then turn to the color chapters to find out your natural spiritual characteristics. If in the case that both letters such as (J)ohn (J)ones vibrate to the same color then this person would be a double Red spectrum spiritual person and the Red color characteristics will have a very strong spiritual effect on this person.

In this world we live in today, I feel that the majority have bypassed and neglected their spiritual center and have not chosen to cultivate it, and that is why we live in such an immoral world. Man has forgotten about his spiritual higher self and decided to cultivate his lower earthy-mental center without first consulting his higher spirit mind. In other words "he has no conscience." History has shown us many tyrants who stole, killed, and maimed millions of people to obtain their earthy material goals. If a person would first consult their higher spiritual mind first for the right decision and get in the habit of acting off of this center then they would not make these horrendous mistakes. History has shown us those that have cultivated their spiritual center such as Jesus and all the saints, popes, priests, nuns, monks, and other spiritually enlightened people who have contributed to others in need such as Gandhi and Mother Theresa.

If everyone would take it upon themselves to cultivate their higher spiritual self just a little more, then the world would be a much better place to live.

Your spiritual center is your imagination center and enthusiasm center and the colors attuned to your spiritual center will stimulate your imagination and enthusiasm! This is, without a doubt, your open-minded center!

The spiritual center is also what I call the supreme optimism center and faith center. When we use or hear sayings such as: "Just do what you feel is right and things will work out" or "Just have faith things will eventually work themselves out." What we are doing is trying to stimulate our higher spiritual mind, which controls our ability to have faith, which sends a message to our lower earthy mind to relax and stop worrying about a problem it is having trouble handling. It's like a cool breeze on a hot night when things seem unbearable. You should use your life-long spiritual colors in your home-decor when you want to create these spiritually energetic uplifting moods, such as happiness, youthfulness, enthusiasm, faithfulness and cleanliness. Using myself as an example, I happen to be a double orange spiritual person, and orange being the creative color (as you will learn in the orange spectrum chapter), whenever I'm being creative, doing oil painting, pottery or any creative constructive endeavor, it puts me in a very youthful, wholesome, cheerful mood. I've truly found out that when I'm being creative in these ways I'm truly at my happiest, and the creative fields are where my imagination and enthusiasm lie.

The best way to uplift one's spirit when one's spirit is low or in a negative spiritual mood, is to get in tune to your daily spiritual color (which I explain in the daily color chapter). Imagine breathing in through your nostrils that color while adding more and more white with it, tinting it down to a lighter tint of that color and imagine this color swirling around your brain and the crown of your head around your spiritual center, and then down through the rest of your body, and see what an uplifting, energetic spirited feeling you receive. Another way to uplift ones spirit is to laugh even if it is a forced phoney (ha-ha) laugh; just keep doing it till you break into a genuine laugh. Laughing has a vibrating effect, just as a jack hammer or vibrating drill, and breaks up solid, hard or bad feelings. Sometimes I do this myself when I get in a bad mood or my temper is starting to boil, and it helps to change my mood instantly. It also makes me feel ten years younger. How can you tell if you're a spiritual type? Spiritual types usually are the type that have a youthful spirited whole-some smile on their face. They also tend to believe in the spiritual world and are very religious, and are usually very kind and concerned about the well being of others. They are also very imaginative and creative. Use your spiritual colors in youthful, vibrant, clean, cheerful tints and sheens in fabrics or paints or whatever materials you use.

Here are some careers in which the spiritual type person excels: Religious, Spiritual (new age), imaginative and creative careers such as teachers, inventors, scientists, artists, fashion designers, interior designers, decorators, hairstylists, and choreographers, etc.. Service oriented fields such as real estate, restaurants, bed and breakfast inns and many more. Healing careers such as Doctors, nursing, etc. Remember the color traits that are attuned to your spiritual center is where your greatest enthusiasm and imagination lie and will be very good career choices.

Spiritual people also make very good leaders because they have the abilities to open other people's minds to worldly ways of looking at different issues.

Sayings that Stimulate Our Spiritual Center

He hath a poor spirit who is not planted above petty wrongs. - Feltham.

A man of right spirit is not a man of narrow and private views, but is greatly interested and concerned for the good of the community to which he belongs, and particularly of the city or village in which he resides, and for the true welfare of the society of which he is a member. - Jonathan Edwards

He that loseth wealth, loseth much: he that loseth friends, loseth more: but he that loseth his spirit, loseth all. - Spanish Maxim

Man's conscience is the oracle of God. - Byron

Conscience is merely our own Judgment of the right or wrong of our actions, and so can never be a safe guide unless enlightened by the word of God. - Tryon Edwards

A good conscience is the palace of Christ: the temple of the Holy Ghost: the paradise of delight: the standing Sabbath of the saints. - Augustine

It is far more important to me to preserve an unblemished conscience than to compass any object however great. - Channing.

Genius may be described as the spirit of discovery. - It is the eye of intellect, and the wing of thought, - It is always in advance of its time - the pioneer for the generation which it precedes. - Simms

When a true genius appears in the world, you may know him by this sign, that the dunces are all in confederacy against him. - Swift

The first and last thing required of genius is the love of truth. - Goethe

Genius finds its own road, and carries its own lamp. - Willmott

Talent, lying in the understanding, is often inherited; genius, being the action of reason and imagination, rarely or never. - Coleridge

Mental Center
Middle Forehead Between Eyebrows

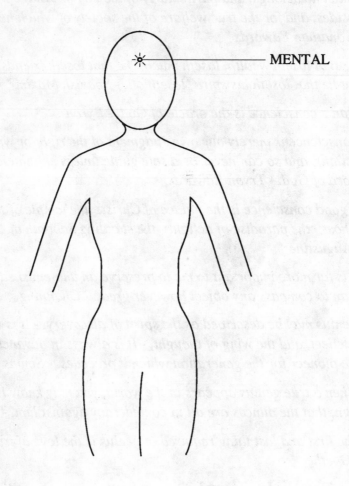

MENTAL

Your Mental Center Letters and Colors

The letters that determine your life-long colors and characteristics of your mental center are the second letters in your first and last names, (J(o)hn D(o)e). Your mental center is located at the center of your forehead as illustrated on page 34. I also call this center your practical, logical, material and earthy mind, because it controls the functions of carrying out the every day logical, simple, or complex analytical problem-solving tasks (how you're getting to work, job decisions, how to make money and how to manage daily decisions).

After your higher spiritual mind decides what's right, your lower logical, earthy mind can go to work to decide how to achieve your worldly or materialistic goals. If used in long term situations such as home and career, your life-long mental colors will look and feel confident, intellectual, logical, practical, reasonable, organized, decisive and positive on and around you. If you're having negative mental thoughts, the effects will be the opposite.

To get back on the right track mentally, just go to the higher spiritual mind, if it's a moral problem and make the right moral decision. If it's an everyday practical decision, just slow down one's mind and ask what is the first, practical, logical step to solving the problem and follow this decision. You will feel your mind start to clear almost immediately. We've all heard sayings such as, "One step at a time" or "Cross that bridge when you get to it."

Those that have problems organizing their life or making or saving enough money, etc., have not cultivated their mental center. Those most associated with having cultivated their mental center are businessmen, educators, scientists, lawyers, doctors, investment advisors, consultants, professional people and practical people in general.

Remember to let your higher spiritual mind first decide or you will probably pay the consequences sooner or later.

Whatever your mental colors are, use them in flat, simple, practical materials, such as cotton and other non-flashy textures and fabrics.

Sayings that Stimulate Our Mental Center

If common sense has not the brilliancy of the sun, it has the fixity of the stars. - Caballero

The crown of all faculties is common sense. It is not enough to do the right thing, it must be done at the right time and place. Talent knows what to do; tact knows when and how to do it. - W. Matthews

Common sense is, of all kinds, the most uncommon. It implies good judgment, sound discretion, and true and practical wisdom applied to common life. - Tryon Edwards

To act with common sense according to the moment, is the best wisdom I know; and the best philosophy is to do one's duties, take the world as it comes, submit respectfully to one's lot; bless the goodness that has given us so much happiness with it, whatever it is; and despise affectation. - Walpole

If a man can have only one kind of sense, let him have common sense. If he has that and uncommon sense too, he is not far from genius.
- H.G. Beecher

One pound of learning requires ten pounds of common sense to apply it.
- Persian Proverb

Common sense is the knack of seeing things as they are, and doing things as they ought to be done. - C.E. Stowe

The intellect of the wise is like glass, it admits the light of heaven and reflects it. - Hare

If we would guide by the light of reason, we must let our minds be bold.
- Justice Brandeis

The mind grows narrow in proportion as the soul grows corrupt.
- Rousseau

Never reason from what you do not know. If you do, you will soon believe what is utterly against reason. - Ramsay

If a man's eye is on the eternal, his intellect will grow. - Emerson

As the soil, however rich it may be, cannot be productive without culture, so the mind without cultivation can never produce good fruit. - Seneca

A man who hasn't bothered to cultivate his common sense, practical mind, will continually be bent over and kicked in the behind by others and also by himself many times. - D.G. Rolliet

What stubbing, plowing, digging, and harrowing is to land, that thinking, reflecting, examining is to the mind. Each has its proper culture: and as the land that is suffered to lie waste and wild for a long time will be overspread with brushwood, brambles, and thorns, which have neither use nor beauty, so there will not fail to sprout up in a neglected, uncultivated mind. A great number of prejudices and absurd opinions, which owe their origin partly to the soil itself, the passions, and imperfections of the mind of man, and partly to those seeds which chance to be scattered in it by every wind of doctrine which the cunning of statesmen, the singularity of pedants, and superstition of fools shall rise. - Berkeley

True wisdom is to know what is best worth knowing, and to do what is best worth doing. - Humphrey

Vocal Center
Base of Throat

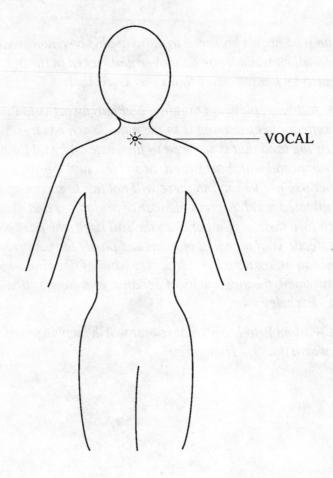

VOCAL

Your Vocal Center Letters and Colors

Your vocal center is located at the base of the throat. The letters that affect and characterize this center is usually the third letter in our names. But the vocal center is also a reflection of the rest of our centers; for instance, if we are in a very emotional mood our voice will sound very emotional. If we are in a very cheerful spiritual mood our voice will vibrate to a cheerful sound. As we all know, certain ethnic people are conditioned to talk in certain ethnic styles, sometimes with a very nasal or guttural quality. Breathing also affects our vocal sounds.

 In the flesh color chapter I mention that it seems to help to have strong flesh color letters ("A," "H," "0," and "V") in a name to become a singer. For those interested in a musical field, read the flesh color chapter.

If you want to sound intellectual and practical align your mental center with your vocal center by concentrating on deriving your thoughts and sounds from these two centers. A person who talks with alot of physical gestures is aligning one's physical center with one's vocal center. A person who talks in a very spirited manner is aligning one's spiritual and vocal centers. Decide on how you wish to sound or project, and concentrate on that center while speaking. Those that have cultivated their vocal center are singers and others who limit their facial and other body gestures while speaking.

Statements that Concern Our Vocal Center

There is no index of character so sure as the voice. - Tancred

How sweetly sounds the voice of a good woman! When it speaks it ravishes all senses. - Massinger

Never is the deep, strong voice of man, or the low, sweet voice of woman, finer than in the earnest but mellow tones of familiar speech, richer than the richest music, which are a delight while they are heard, which linger still upon the ear in softened echoes, and which when they have ceased, come, long after, back to memory, like the murmurs of a distant hymn. - Henry Giles

The sound must seem an echo to the sense. - Pope

To a nice ear the quality of a voice is singularly affecting. Its depth seems to be allied to feeling: at least the contralto notes alone give an adequate sense of pathos. They are born near the heart. - Tuckerman

How deep is the magic of sound may be learned by breaking some sweet verses into prose. The operation has been compared to gathering dew-drops, which shine like jewels upon the flower, but run into water in the hand. The elements remain, but the sparkle is gone. - Willmott

There is in souls a sympathy with sounds, and as the wind is pitched the ear is pleased with melting airs or martial, brisk or grave: Some chord in unison with what we hear is touched within us, and the heart replies. - Cowper

Physical Center
Middle of Chest

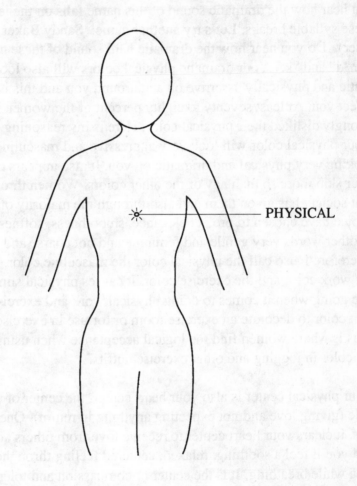

PHYSICAL

The Physical Center Letters and Colors

The physical center is located at the center of the chest (as illustrated on page 41). The letters that come right after your syllable breaks in your name are your physical letters (Ro-(b)ert Red-(m)an) the "b" and "m". I also call the physical color letters your dramatic color letters because you can hear how the dramatic sound of this name falls on the letters right after these syllable breaks. Let's try another name: Sandy Baker, (San-(d)e Ba-(k)er). Do you hear how the dramatic hard sound of these names fall on the "d" and "k." Your dramatic physical colors will also look and feel dramatic and physically assertive on and around you and this is how they will affect you. At least seventy to eighty percent of the women I interviewed strongly disliked their physical color. Here is my reasoning on why this is. Your physical color will look very aggressive and masculine as well as looking very physical and dramatic on you. It also appears coarse against your skin more so than any of the other colors. Women through the roles that society has given them and also through the majority of their own choice have chosen to project elegance, smoothness, softness, and relaxed. In other words very gentle and feminine and not coarse and aggressive. Therefore I also call the physical color the masculine color. I also call it the work color and the exercise color. It causes physical stimulation to get one going when it comes to doing physical work and exercise. It is the best color to decorate an exercise room or for use in exercise garments. This is where women find the logical acceptance when using their physical color in jogging and other exercise outfits.

Your physical center is also your heart center, the center of unconditional love (giving love and not expecting anything in return). Once you can do this, it clears your heart center to receive love from others and yourself, and you'll feel a soothing, relaxed, centered feeling throughout your chest area while breathing. It is the center of compassion and tolerance and unpretentiousness; and when you're able to achieve this state of unconditional love, the harsh qualities of your dramatic physical center colors become more comfortable. You'll no longer feel so aggressive and dramatic. You will have become more unpretentious, honest, humble, and handsome. When you have achieved this, you can then use your physical colors in softer tints, hues, and shades in fabrics and environments.

Those who are usually thought of as cultivating their physical center are weight lifters, bodybuilders, athletes, dancers and anyone that engages in a lot of physical activity, or those that are very dramatic in nature. These types usually excel in the field of drama, acting and entertainment fields. Use your physical color in dramatic, dynamic, warm tints and hues, shades, and textures.

During a recent television program, a weightlifter was placed in front of the color pink (elegance). He stared at it for several minutes and then lifted 250 lbs. But when placed before the color blue (spirit) he proceeded to lift 325 lbs. (an increase of 75 lbs.)!

Sayings that Stimulate the Physical Center

The wise, for cure, on exercise depend. Better to hunt in fields for health unbought than fee the doctor for a nauseous draught. - Dryden

Health is the vital principle of bliss; and exercise, of health. - Thomson

The only way for a rich man to be healthy is by exercise and abstinence, to live as if he was poor; which are esteemed the worst parts of poverty. - Sir W. Temple

Inactivity, supineness, and effeminacy have ruined more constitutions than were ever destroyed by excessive labors. Moderate exercise and toil, so far from prejudicing, strengthen and consolidate the body. - Richard Rush

Control Center
Upper Solar Plexus

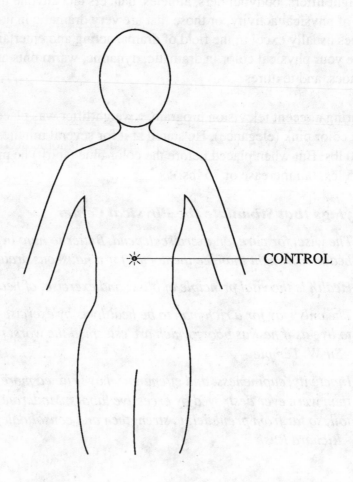

CONTROL

Your Control Center Letters and Colors

The control center is located above the navel, at your solar plexus, (illustrated on page 44). The letters in your names that determine your life-long control center colors and characteristics are the letters right before your syllable breaks. For example: ((R(o)-bert B(u)-ca(n)-on or Sa(n)-dra Lau(r)-en), where the sound hangs on in a controlling manner, right before your dramatic syllable breaks. Our control center is where our self-control originates. I also call our control center our power center, our regal-royal center, our "no-nonsense" center or "firm-in-opinion" center. When one is in control, one also has the ability to say "no" to others when one decides that they disagree or will not act or respond in certain situations. One also has the feeling of regality, royalty and stateliness so your control colors are definitely your "Power" colors in this sense. In home decor, to obtain the mood of formal regality or refinement in a room or rooms, use your life-long regal colors to achieve this mood. Your control colors and textures should be used in very refined, regal colors and fabrics. If a person has problems with their self-control they will have problems with compulsive behavior, an addictive personality, excessive fear, or anger, etc.

If you are an individual who often feels powerless, inferior, or the ability to demand what you believe you deserve when you come into contact with others, then you need to get in touch with your control center and colors. Whether it concerns money or respect, if you are always doing for others (subservient), you need to break these habits. Remember, your control center is the center of dignity, respect, refinement, and power. Try getting in touch with your daily control center color (which I explain in the daily color chapter) and the traits of that color on a daily basis for a few weeks. By doing this, you will start to feel and see yourself acting very regal and refined.

You'll start to notice others starting to pay more attention and respect towards you. People tend to be drawn to those that project a sense of power and refinement and tend to offer their services to these dignified persons.

This is the center that powerful people in high positions have cultivated. Top executives are not timid, they have the ability to project control color traits. Learn to build your own power center, and you'll be able to command more of what you deserve. Other careers in which those that have cultivated their control traits excell: Posture and image consultants, models, excessive/compulsive behavior consultants, art and antique historians, corporate spokespersons, press secretaries, and many other fields where there is a very strong need for poise and control, such as brain surgeons, ballet dancers, or any career where the elements of control, refinement are needed.

I have also discovered that this center is where we will have a controlling affect on others; for example, if you are a blue control person then you will have a controlling affect in an emotional way on a blue emotional person or if that person is a blue mental person you will have a mental controlling affect and so on with other blue center persons. On the other hand, if you happen to be, a yellow emotional person, then a yellow control person will control you emotionally. So whenever you control or are controlled, don't let it become an abusive situation, don't let it get out of hand, have fun with it, but don't abuse this power.

Statements That Stimulate The Control Center

Who to himself is law, no law doth need. - Chapman

No conflict is so severe as his who labors to subdue himself.
- Thomas A. Kempis

It is the man who is cool and collected, who is master of his countenance, his voice, his actions, his gestures, of every part, who can work upon others at his pleasure. - Diderot

Be noble-minded! Our own heart and not other men's opinions of us, forms our true honor. - Schiller

No man is free who cannot command himself. - Pythagoras

Self-respect, - that corner-stone of all virtue. - Sir John Herscel

Emotional Center
Middle of Abdomen

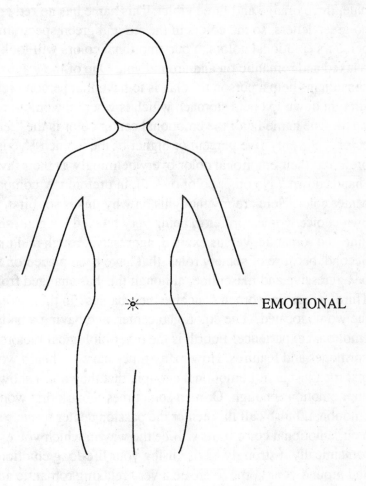

EMOTIONAL

Emotional Center Letters and Colors

Your emotional center is located at the center of your abdomen. The letters that correspond to your emotional center are, believe it or not, the color letters which you do not have in your name. For example, "Sandra Piper." As you can see this name has two yellow letters, two flesh, one blue, three orange and three violet. This name has no red color letters and no green letters, so the colors in the red and green spectrums would be this person's emotional colors. Your emotional colors will look and feel relaxed and romantic on and around you. One of the ways that stress consultants help a person to relax is to have that person breathe slowly straight down to one's stomach which is where the emotional center is located. One name I call the emotional center color is the "feminine center color." Seventy-five percent or higher of the women I've interviewed, preferred their emotional color overwhelmingly as their favorite color, "hands down." No other color overall, in preference, compared to this center color. Here are my thoughts on why this is so: First, it is by their own choice women prefer to being very relaxed, elegant, smooth, feminine and romantic, versus excited, aggressive, rough and masculine. Second, because of society roles, that have been placed on women not to be aggressive and masculine, although this has changed from time to time. Third, where do women conceive their babies? In their wombs! Where is the womb located? The emotional center, and having a baby is a very emotional experience! Fourth is the other biological factors of women - hormones and features. How many times have we heard women remark that men just aren't emotional enough, that they don't show or express their emotions enough. Or men sometimes remark that women are overly emotional. I also call this center the passion center or the romantic center. Your emotional color traits will be the way in which you express yourself romantically. I strongly advise using your life-long emotional colors in and around your home to create a very relaxing romantic atmosphere. Use soft-flowing and romantic colors and textures.

Note: If you have all seven of the letter colors in your name, such as Nancy Waterfield, then your emotional color will be in the gray color spectrum.

Your emotional center is also the contentment center. How can one be really relaxed, if one is not really content? I do a little exercise to relax myself. I say aloud, while breathing air in and out, straight down to my abdomen, seven times, these words:

I feel relaxed - I feel content.

I feel content - I feel relaxed.

I feel relaxed - I feel content.

I feel soulful.

Why then, do I feel soulful? What happens to us when we become relaxed and content? We become very soulful, and this usually leads to a nice soulful belly laugh!

Note: I've also noticed that a substantial number of women like to combine their emotional colors with their sexual colors.

Those that have cultivated their emotional center traits will look and project very romantic and relaxed.

Careers that the emotionally cultivated excel in are: communication specialists, designers of environments that create a relaxful and romantic atmosphere.

Sayings That Stimulate the Emotional Center

Resign every forbidden joy; restrain every wish that is not referred to God's will; banish all eager desires, all anxiety; desire only the will of God; seek him alone and supremely, and you will find peace. - Fenelon

If you are but content you have enough to live upon with comfort. - Plautus

The taste for emotion may become a dangerous taste; we should be very cautious how we attempt to squeeze out of human life more ecstasy and paroxysm that it can well afford. - Sydney Smith

A contented mind is the greatest blessing a man can enjoy in this world; and if, in the present life, his happiness arises from the subduing of his desires, it will arise in the next from the gratification of them. - Addison

Alternate rest and labor long endure. - Ovid

Emotion, whether of ridicule, anger, or sorrow, whether raised at a puppetshow, a funeral, or a battle, is your grandest of levelers. The man who would be always superior should be always apathetic. - Bulwer

Submission is the only reasoning between a creature and its maker and contentment in his will is the best remedy we can apply to misfortunes. - Sir W. Temple

Emotion turning back on itself, and not leading on to thought or action, is the element of madness. - J. Sterling

It is right to be contented with what we have, never with what we are. - MacKintosh

There are pauses amidst study, and even pauses of seeming idleness, in which a process goes on which may be likened to the digestion of food. In those seasons of repose, the powers are gathering their strength for new efforts; as land which lies fallow recovers itself for tillage. - J. W. Alexander

By starving emotions we become humorless, rigid and stereotyped; by repressing them we become literal, reformatory and holier-than- thou; encouraged, they perfume life; discouraged, they poison it. - Dr. Joseph Collins

I never complained of my condition but once, said an old man - when my feet were bare, and I had no money to buy shoes; but I met a man without feet, and became contented. -

All work and no rest takes the spring and bound out of the most vigorous life. - Time spent in judicious resting is not time wasted, but time gained. - M.B. Grier

All loving emotions, like plants, shoot up most rapidly in the tempestuous atmosphere of life. - Richter

The contented man is never poor; the discontented never rich.
He who is not contented with what he has, would not be contented with
what he would like to have.

Ride your emotions as the shallop rides the waves; don't get upset
among them. There are people who enjoy getting swamped emotionally
just as, incredibly, there are people who enjoy getting drunk.
- Mary Austin

Contentment is natural wealth, luxury is artificial poverty. - Socrates

Rest is not quitting the busy career; rest is the fitting of self to its
sphere. - J. Dwight

Sexual Center

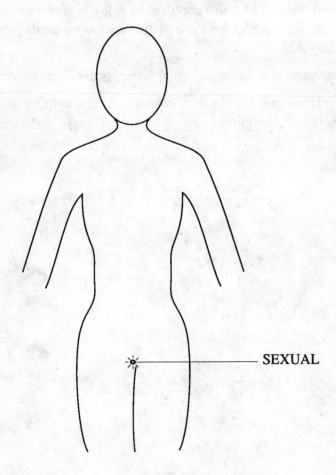

SEXUAL

The Sexual Center Letters and Colors

The letters that determine your sexual colors are the last letters in your first and last names such as Paul(a) D(o)e - pronounced Paul-l(a) D(o) (the "e" in the last name is silent.) So this is a double flesh sexual person. For Robert Little (pronounced Ro-ber(t) Lit-t(l)) the green and yellow color spectrums would apply. Your sexual colors will stimulate you sexually, and the characteristics of your sexual colors will be how you generally project sexually. Your sexual center is also used for releasing and eliminating waste and toxins; and if we think about it, in order to enjoy or project sexually we must have the ability to release our built up stresses - spiritual, mental or emotional. We must learn to release. This is why one can have greater sexual release when one has sex with someone that they sincerely like, spiritually, mentally, physically and emotionally; not just for physical, security or monetary reasons. The more inhibitions that build up, the harder it is to release sexually. Just take, for example, people who have been raped or abused; they have to learn to release the past and get in touch with themselves and their centers. You've heard sayings such as "you have to accentuate the positive and eliminate the negative". So first find yourself someone with whom you can relate to, in as many ways as possible to your centers, which I discuss in Chapter 10, so the chance for commitment and marriage can be greater and your sexual experiences will be more satisfying. Your sexual colors and textures should be sultry, silky, suave, seductive and transparent fabrics that have the ability to drape and hang nicely on the curves of your body.

Another way of getting in touch with your sexual center is to breathe deeply from your sexual center while making rich, resonant sounds of the letters that are attuned to your daily sexual center-colors (Chapter 8). What you are doing with this exercise is resounding or revibrating or, in other words, tuning or bringing to life this vibrating force. Those that have cultivated their sexual center usually have a sexy walk, a sexy smile, and a sexy voice and will tend to wear sensual clothing (the suave type).

Statements on Sex

The principal reason for sex deification is loss of belief of God. Once men lose God, they lose the purpose of life; and when the purpose of living is forgotten, the universe becomes meaningless. Man then tries to forget his emptiness in the intensity of a momentary experience. - Fulton J. Sheen

Sex is an much psychological as physical. Certainly love is much more than physical sex appeal. - Harold H. Titus

Sex has become one of the most discussed subjects of modern time. The Victorians pretended it did not exist; the moderns pretend that nothing else exists. - Fulton J. Sheen

Conclusion

Just about all names will have more than one color in the same center. For example: Gina Messer. This person's spiritual colors are blue and green. She could use either blue and green colors separately in a room to bring about a youthful, spiritual effect or she might like to mix the two to get a blue-green color, to achieve this mood. The color yellow is her mental, control and physical color, and it will have a combination effect. If she wants to decorate a room with both a sexual and an emotional effect, she would use flesh and orange for the sexual and colors in the red spectrum for the emotional effect. Because she has no red letters in her name, making her a red, relaxed emotional person. In the color fan I have included not only true hue colors for your color fan, but also combination colors such as blue-greens, yellow-greens, purple-reds, etc. Feel free to add as many color combinations to your color fan as you wish. The more colors you add the better chance you have of tuning into your colors more precisely.

6
The Colors and Their Characteristics

6
The Colors and
Their Characteristics

Flesh Spectrum – *Harmony - Organization - Practicality*
Violet Spectrum – *Culture - Writing - Psychic*
Red Spectrum – *Romance - Physical Life Forces - Elegance*
Orange Spectrum – *Creativity - Kindness - Versatility*
Yellow Spectrum – *Science - Education - Cheerfulness*
Green Spectrum – *Poise - Balance - Justice*
Blue Spectrum – *Spiritual - Imaginative - Dependable*
White – *Holiness - Giving - Healing*
Gray – *Neutrality, Mutual Agreement - Separator*
Black – *Rest - Consuming - New Beginnings*

Colors have been studied and written about ever since the dawn of civilization. Biblical records have the first order of God, "Let there be light," and other quotes: "Though ye shall be as Red as Crimson, I shall wash ye as White as Snow". Quotes from Jesus: "I am the light of the world. He who follows me does not walk in the darkness, but will have the "Light" of life". From the first epistle of St. John the Apostle: "God is light, and the message which we have heard from him and announce to you is this, that God is "light", and in Him is no darkness at all. If we say that we have fellowship with Him and walk in darkness, we lie, and are not practicing the truth. But if we walk in the "Light" as He also is in the "Light" we have fellowship with one another and the hand of Jesus Christ, His Son, cleanses us from all sin." Quotes from persons who have died and returned from out-of-body experiences usually talk about the brilliant light and color that they experience, and some who say they've met Jesus or God, talk about Him standing in beautiful light and color. Others who have had bad out-of-body experiences have talked of the darkness of hell. Many historical persons and civilizations have discussed and written of the spiritual meanings and effects of light and color such as: Beethoven, Segovia, Richard Wagner, Raphael, Goethe, Ravel, Debussy, Scriabin, the ancient Chaldeans, etc.. Spiritual color analysts talk of the seven colors in relation to the seven archangels.

In the next chapters I will outline the spiritual characteristics of these colors and how they affect us. I've also read many statements from interior designers who make the statement that colors are the most personal and revealing expressions of a person's personality, but after just about every one of these statements, they then go into a general description of how the color red or blue or yellow affects us in general. Decorators and designers should try to learn how each and every color affects each individual.

Flesh Spectrum
Harmony - Organization - Practicality

The flesh spectrum ranges from light off-white beige, tans, browns, to deep, dark chocolate browns. The letters that harmonize with the flesh spectrum are "A," "H," "O," and "V". The flesh spectrum is the spectrum of organization, unity, and harmony. The rest of the positive traits of the spectrum: morality, compensation, practicality, perception, coordination (organization), articulateness, unity (mind-body-soul), universality, and introspective. The negative traits are: disorderliness, intolerance, inconsiderateness, inconsistency, confusion, idolatry. In order to get a true hue flesh color, one would mix equal parts of true yellow, true red and true blue together and come up with a coppery flesh color. If one desired a light beige color or light skin color, one would mix white with this combination. For a dark brown, one would mix black with it. This is the color spectrum which I feel Sir Isaac Newton referred to when speaking of Indigo. This spectrum is the combining of all the colors: the yellow of intellect, the red of physical, the blue of soul (mind, body, and soul.) Flesh spectrum people who cultivate this spectrum are very good organizers; they're very practical. I also call this spectrum the musical and financial spectrum. The musical field is a natural career field for those that have cultivated their flesh traits. If we think about what it takes to be a good singer, musician or composer, it takes harmony - that is the harmonizing of one's mental thoughts, ones emotions, and one's physical-vocal chords. When one does this, it all comes together to bring about clarification - a clear, beautifully organized voice or sounds or statement (fluency). One has to really feel, think and believe in one's message to accomplish this. Flesh cultivated people are very good money makers, they are very frugal with money, they hate to waste money, they are able to organize in a very practical way how they will go about making or managing their money. They hate to be disorganized. They are usually very fastidiously neat. Flesh people can get along with all kinds of people and all situations. They are very confident. They feel as if they can accomplish anything they set their minds on. Remember they have it all together - mind, body, and soul. They have the ability to remember past experiences and results and make practical decisions on this ability to recall, store, and organize these experiences. Flesh people must guard against becoming arrogant and overly confident. Extreme cases of this will result in one becoming like a demi-God or the feeling that one is God himself.

Notice the many famous people who cultivated their flesh musical traits and notice where the dramatics fall on the flesh letters in most cases with flesh musical people - "A," "H," "O," and "V."

	Pronunciation
Andre Previn	(A)ndr-(a) Pre-(v)in
Antonio Stradivarius	(A) n-t(o)-ne-(o) Str(a)d-a-(v)(a)ri-(a)s
Amadeus Mozart	W(o)lfg(a)ng (A)m(a)-d(a)-(a)s M(o)z-(a)rt
Andrea Segovia	(A)n-dra-(a) S(a)-g(o)-(v)ee-(a)
Aaron Copeland	(A)rr-(o)n C(o)pe-l(a)nd
Burt Bacarach	Burt B(a)-k(a)-r(a)k
Barry Manilow	B(a)r-e M(a)n-(a)-l(o)
Claudio Monteverde	Kl(a)-de-(o) M(o)n-t(a)-(v)erd(a)
Diana Ross	Di-(a)n-(a) R(o)ss
Dion Warwick	De-(o)n W(a)r-wick

Diahhn Carrol	Di-(a)n K(a)r-(o)l
David Brubeck	D(a)-(v)id Bru-beck
Diane Renay	Di-(a)n R(a)-n(a)
Elvis Aaron Presley	El-(v)(a)s (A)rr-(o)n Pres-lee
Enrico Caruso	(O)n-re-k(o) K(a)ru-s(o)
Frank Albert Sinatra	(Fr(a)nk (A)l-bert S(a)-n(a)-tr-(a)
Frankie Avalon	Fr(a)n-ke (A)-(v)(a)-l(o)n
Fabian	F(a)-be-(a)n
Howard Keel	(H)(o)-w(a)rd Keel
Harry Richmond	(H)(a)r-re Ric(h)-m(o)nd
Harold Arlen	(H)(a)r-(o)ld (A)r-l(a)n
Herbie Hancock	(H)er-bee (H)(a)n-k(o)ck
Hank Williams	(H)(a)n-k Wil-y(a)ms
Henry Mancini	(H)en-ree M(a)n-c-nee
Irving Berlin	Er-(v)een Ber-lin
Issac Hayes	Iss-(a) c (H)(a)-z
John (Johnathan) Lennon	J(o)(h)-n or J(o)(h)n-(a)-t(h)(a)n Len-(o)n
John Darden	J(o)(h)n D(a)r-den
Julio Iglesias	(H)ulee-(o) E-gl(a)-s(ha)
Jerry (Jerald) Vale	Ger-ee or Ger-(a)ld (V)(a)-le
Johnny Cash	(J(o)(h)n-ee K(a)s(h)
Ludwig Van Beethoven	Lud-(v)ig (V)(o)n B(a)-t(o)-(v)en
Luciano Pavarotti	Lu-c(h)ee-(o)n-(o) P(a)-(v)(a)r(o)-t(a)
Lena Horne	Leen-(a) (H)(o)rn
Lionel Richie	Li-(a)-nel Ric(h)-(h)ee
Mahalia Jackson	M(a)-(h)(a)-l(a) J(a)k-s(o)n
Martha Vandella	M(a)rt(h)-(a) (V)(a)n-del-(a)
Mario Lanza	M(a)r-e-(o) L(a)n-z(a)
Marvin Hamlish	M(a)r-(v)in (H)(a)m-lis(h)
Miles Davis	Mi-(a)lez D(a)-(v)is
Nat (Nathanial) King Cole	N(a)-t(h)(a)n-(a)l King K(o)le
Neal Sedaka	Ne-(a)l S(a)-d(a)k-(a)
Olivia Newton John	(O)-li(v)-(v)ee-(a) Newt(o)n J(o)(h)n
Oliver	(O)-li-(v)er
Paul Anka	P(a)u-l (A)n-k(a)
Paul Macarthney	P(a)u-l M(a)-k(a)rt-nee

Richard Strauss	(V)ic(h)-(a)rd Str(a)(a)ss
Richard Wagner	(V)ic(h)-(a)rd (V)(a)g-ner
Sylvia	Sil-(v)ee-(a)
Sam Cooke	S(a)m K(o)(o)k
Tom (Thomas) Jones	T(h)(o)m-(a)s J(o)n-z
Victor Damone	(V)ik-t(o)r D(a)m(o)n

Other famous flesh musical people:
(A)lex(a)nder Nik(o)l(a)ie(v)ic(h) Scri(a)bin
(A)nit(a) B(a)ker
(A)nt(o)n D(v)(o)r(a)k
(A)nt(o)ni(o) (V)i(v)(a)ldi
(A)nt(o)ny(o) D(o)nt(o)ny(o)
B(a)rb(a)r(a) Lewis [B(a)r-br(a) Lu-(a)s]
Be(v)erly Sills
Del S(h)(a)nn(o)n
Di(o)n D(a)muc(h)i
Fr(a)nki (V)(a)lli
Fr(a)nz Sc(h)ubert
Fr(a)nz J(o)sef (H)(a)yden
Frederic C(h)(o)pin
Gust(a)(v) M(a)(h)ler
I(v)(o) P(o)g(o)relic(h)
J(o)(h)(a)nn Seb(a)sti(a)n B(a)c(h)
J(o)(h)(a)nness (Br(a)(h)ms
J(o)(h)n C(o)rigli(a)n(o)
Lut(h)er (V)(a)ndr(o)ss
Na(o)mi Judd [Ni-(o)me J(a)dd]
(O)sc(a)r (H)(a)mmerstein
(O)tis Reddins [(O)t- (a)s Redd-ing]
Pi(o)tr Tc(h)(a)ik(o)(v)sky
Ric(h)(a)rd R(o)dgers
(V)(a)n Clyeburn
(V)l(a)dimir (H)(o)r(o)witz
Wyn(o)nn(a) Judd [Wi-n(o)nn-(a) J(a)dd], and many more.

Sayings That Stimulate Flesh Traits

Order is a lovely nymph, the child of beauty and wisdom; her attendants are comfort, neatness, and activity; her abode is the valley of happiness; she is always to be found when sought for, and never appears so lovely as when contrasted with her opponent, disorder. - Johnson

We do not keep the outward form of order, where there is deep disorder in the mind. - Shakespeare

Order is heaven's first law. - Pope

He who has no taste for order, will often wrong in his judgement, and seldom considerate or conscientious is his actions. - Lavater

Order is the sanity of the mind, the health of the body, the peace of the city, the security of the state. - As the beams to a house, as the bones to the body, so is order to all things. - Southey

The heavens themselves, the planets, and this centre, observe degree, priority and place, insisture, course, proportion, season, form, office, and custom, in all line of order. - Shakespeare

Have a time and place for everything, and do everything in its time and place, and you will not only accomplish more, but have far more leisure than those who are always hurrying, as if vainly attempting to overtake time that had been lost. - Tryon Edwards

Violet Spectrum
Culture - Writing - Psychic

Violet spectrum letters are "B," "I," "P," and "W". The violet spectrum ranges from very light lavenders to purple, from true hue violet to dark deep violets. The violet color spectrum is the spectrum of "pure idealism", royalty, regality, civilization and power. The other positive traits are: maturity (of desires), dedication, intuition (psychic), tasteful (in the arts), cultured, self-sacrifice (self-denial). The negative traits are: fanaticism, superiority, monopolization, treachery, snobbishness, pompousness, domination. Violet people can be very dedicated to whatever they engage in: their career, their employers, their loved ones, and will self-sacrifice themselves out of dedication. If we think about people who are dedicated and have pure ideals, they are the ones who can truly hold their heads up high in dignity in winning or losing. We've all heard the expression: "Well, at least you truly tried." Violet people usually don't lose because they "see things through." Jesus paid the supreme self-sacrifice and now He sits on a "regal throne". Anyone who achieves anything of value does so through dedications. Power comes from these traits of dedication and sacrifice; after which a person can be pleased with their efforts. Violet people are lovers of the arts. They have a natural ability to turn something that is raw, materialistic, mundane or vulgar into something refined and dignified, a work of art. Those that have cultivated the positive traits have what we call "real class." Violet people also fit the quote "the pen is mightier than the sword." This can be observed by the many famous writers, poets, and publishers in the literature field, which is a natural career field for cultivated violet people, such as:

Alex Haley (emotional violet person)
(B)ar(b)ra Taylor (B)radford
Edgar R(i)ce (B)urroughs
Ed(i)th Jones Ne(w)(b)old (W)harton
El(i)za(b)eth (B)arrett (B)ro(w)ning
El(i)za(b)eth (B)o(w)en
Ernest Hemming(w)ay
Her(b)ert George (W)ells - H.G. Wells
James Joyce - emotional violet person
John Keats - emotional violet person
John Stanley (W)(e)yman - e sounds to (i)
Joseph (P)ul(i)tzer
Noah (W)e(b)ster
(P)ercy (B)ysshe Shelley
Ray (B)rad(b)ury
Ro(b)ert (B)ro(w)ning
Ro(b)ert Lou(i)s Stevenson
Rudyard K(i)(p)ling
Samuel Langhorne Clemens - Mark T(w)ain

S(i)r (W)alter Scott
Tom (W)olfe
U(p)ton S(i)nclair
(W)alt (W)h(i)tman
(W)(i)lla Cather
(W)(i)lliam Faulkner
(W)(i)lliam (P)enn
(W)(i)lliam Randolph Hearst
(W)(i)lliam Shakes(p)eare
(W)(i)lliam Taylor Adams
(W)(i)lliam Vaughan Moody
(W)(i)lliam (W)ords(w)orth

Violet people must guard from becoming too fanatical in seeking power through monopolization for this leads to treachery.

Violet people seem to be very psychic. This is a field which I plan to study in greater depth.

It has been stated that many of the astronauts that returned to Earth after travel in outer space had higher levels of intuition and psychic experiences. In fact, one of the astronauts, Edgar D. M(i)tchell, has written a book on psychic research and exploration. In the case of astronauts I have a few different theories on why, if in fact they did return to Earth with stronger psychic powers, and one of those theories has to do with their exposure to stronger amounts of ultra "violet" light. Besides, a trip to outer space in itself has to be a very mind expanding experience!

Violet people also excel in image consulting fields such as posture teachers, modeling agency instructors, photographic image professionals, etc. When I look in the advertising section of a telephone directory, I see a very high percentage of the names advertised in these fields have many violet letters in their names. In a photographic book compiled of many famous pictures taken by some of the most famous photographers, out of the seventy-nine photographers listed fifty-three had strong violet letters in their names. The rest were violet emotional persons, and to many photographers taking photographs is a very emotional experience, especially when one is trying to catch emotional moments on film.

Sayings That Stimulate Violet Traits

Nations, like individuals, live or die, but civilization cannot perish.
- Mazzini

Human beings . . . should become civilized, that is, so related to each other that their thinking is a concerted attempt to reach common answers to common problems. They should practice a friendliness of the mind. Violence . . . is savagery. Civilization is reasonableness.
- Alexander Meiklejohn

A sufficient and sure method of civilization is the influence of good women. - Emerson

The old Hindoo saw, in his dream, the human race led out to its various fortunes. First, men were in chains, that went back to an iron hand. Then he saw them led by threads from the brain, which went upward to an unseen hand. The first was despotism, iron, and ruling by force. The last was civilization ruling by ideas. - Wendell Phillips

It is very rare to find ground which produces nothing. If it is not covered with flowers, fruit trees, and grains, it produces briars and pines. It is the same with man; if he is not virtuous, he becomes vicious. - Bruyere

It matters little whether a man be mathematically, or philologically, or artistically cultivated, so he be but cultivated. - Goethe

Cultivation to the mind, is as necessary as food to the body. - Cicero

We never reach our ideals, whether of mental or moral improvement, but the thought of them shows us our deficiencies, and spurs us on to higher and better things. - Tryon Edwards

Every life has its actual blanks which the ideal must fill up, or which else remain bare and profitless forever. - J.W. Howe

*The best and noblest lives are those which are set toward high ideals.
And the higher the noblest ideal that any man can have is Jesus of
Nazareth. - Rene Almeras*

Red Spectrum
Romance - Physical Life Forces - Elegance

The red spectrum consists of the pink reds (reds tinted with white), true
hue reds, and dark wine reds (reds that are shaded with black). Find out
where your red letters "C," "J," "Q," and "X" are in your name and what
energy center they correspond to and then apply the following red attributes and characteristics to that center or centers. Red is the romantic color,
and it's also the physical color. Here are the attributes to the red spectrum
that fall under those two basic characteristics. The positive ones are beauty
of manner(elegance), gratefulness (thankfulness), honesty (sincerity),
mercifulness (compassion), persistence (tenaciousness), valor (courage),
benevolence (friendliness), and physical life energy.

The negative traits of the red spectrum are self-pity, physical egotism,
rudeness (coarseness), excessive carnal desire, savageness (barbaric),
jealousy (envy), pitilessness (lack of compassion), and impulsiveness
(impatience).

People who have cultivated the positive traits of the red spectrum excel in
the medical profession, medical research and biology, and any subject
pertaining to the study of the physical life forces. Red people need physical proof. Red people make excellent mechanics. Red people are of a
romantic nature. They write romantic novels, letters, buy flowers for loved
ones, go to romantic places, decorate romantic interiors. The red spectrum
is the color spectrum that is liked quite frequently by women, as we all
know women have a romantic nature. If you don't believe this, just look at
all the romantic novels purchased by women versus men. Red people must
be aware not to judge just on physical appearances alone. They must also
guard against being too impulsive in their actions, like driving a car too
fast, or jumping into a love relationship too quickly. Red people are
subject to bad love experiences at times because of some of the above.

Check the letter-color chart and see where your romance originates. Are you a spiritually, physically, sexually, or emotionally etc., red person?

Famous People with Red Attributes:
(C)harlie (C)haplin
(C)haro
Edward (J)enner - English surgeon and inventor of vaccination
Hebert Spen(c)er (J)ennings - American biologist and author
(J)oan Baez
(J)ack Lemmon
(J)ac(q)ueline Kennedy Onassis
(J)ames (J)oyce
(J)anice (J)oplin
(J)ane Fonda
(J)es-(s)e (J)ackson - s sounds to c in first name
(J)es(s)e Owens - s sounds to c in first name
(J)ohnny Carson
(J)ohn Kennedy
(J)ohn Lennon
(J)ohnny Mathis
(J)onas Salk - Developer of polio vaccine
(J)ulie Andrews
Lu(c)ille Ball
Natalie Wood - emotional red person
Pierre (C)urrie - c is pronounced as a q
Walter Reed - emotional red person

Sayings That Stimulate Red Traits

Love gives itself: it is not bought. - Longfellow

Love which is only an episode in the life of man, is the entire history of woman's life. - Mad. de Staël

The motto of chivalry is also the motto of wisdom: to serve all, but love only one. - Balzac

The treasures of the deep are not so precious as are the concealed comforts of a man locked up in woman's love. - Middleton

Affections, like the conscience, are rather to be led than drawn: and 'tis to be feared, they that marry where they do not love, will love where they do not marry. - Fuller

We are shaped and fashioned by what we love. - Goethe

When the mind loses its feeling for elegance, it grows corrupt and grovelling, and seeks in the crowd what ought to be found at home. - Landor

The heart of him who truly loves is a paradise on earth: he has God in himself, for God is love. - Lamennais

I am not one of those who do not believe in love at first sight, but I believe in taking a second look. - H. Vincent

I have enjoyed the happiness of the world: I have lived and loved. - Schiller

Let grace and goodness be the principal loadstone of thy affections. For love which hath ends, will have an end: whereas that which is founded on true virtue, will always continue. - Dryden

Passion may be blind: but to say that love is, is a libel and a lie. - Nothing is more sharp-sighted or sensitive than true love, in discerning, as by an instinct, the feeling of another. - W.H. Davis

Love is an image of God, and not a lifeless image, but the living essence of the divine nature which beams full of all goodness. - Luther

Absence in love is like water upon fire: a little quickens, but much extinguishes it. - Hannah More

It is better to have loved and lost, than not to love at all. - Tennyson

The plainest man that can convince a woman that he is really in love with her, has done more to make her in love with him than the handsomest man, if he can produce no such conviction. For the love of woman is a shoot, not a seed, and flourishes most vigorously only when ingrafted on that love which is rooted in the breast of another. - Colton

The soul of woman lives in love. - Lydia H. Sigourney

*Elegance is something more than ease - more than a freedom from
awkwardness and restraint. - It implies a precision, a polish, and a
sparkling which is spirited, yet delicate. - Hazlitt*

Orange Spectrum
Creativity - Kindness - Versatility

The orange letters are "D," "K," "R," and "Y". The color orange is
derived from mixing equal parts of red and yellow - red the love color and
yellow the intelligent color. This makes orange the love/wisdom color.
The orange spectrum ranges from light peach orange to true hue orange to
dark earthy orange rusts. Orange is also the creative color. The positive
traits of the orange spectrum are creativity, joyfulness, inspiration enthusiasm, venturesome, self-assurance, speculation, versatile, repentance, kindness (warm heartedness). The negative traits are boastfulness, dishearted-
ness, unpleasantness, despair (depression), destructiveness, exhibitionism,
flamboyance, and overly versatile and venturesome in too many ventures.

People who have cultivated the positive side will be basically very kind,
creative, and constructive. Those that have cultivated the negative will be
just the opposite, very cruel, uncreative, and destructive. Orange people
excel in any field where their creativeness can be channeled. For example,
orange physical people are very creative with their hands. They are natural
sculptures, potters, artists, and wood carvers, athletes, etc., especially
when they have blue letters ("G," "N," and "U") for imagination support-
ing their orange creative letters "D," "K," "R," and "Y".

Following is a list of some famous orange physical people. Notice that
most of them also have the blue spectrum letters. Notice how the dramatic
orange letters fall right after syllable breaks.

	Pronunciation
Andre Derain	An-(d)ra De-(r)an
Camille Pissaro	Ke-me-(y)a Pe-sa-(r)o
Claude Monet	Klo-(d) Mo-na
Diego Rivera	De-a-go Re-va-(r)a
Edouard Manet	A-(d)war Ma-na
El Greco	El Gra-(k)o
Francisco De Goya	Fran-sis-(k)o (D)e Go-(y)a
Frederick Remington	Fred-(r)ick Rem-en-ton
Georges Seurat	Zhorzh Su-(r) a
Giorgio De Chirico	Jor-jo (D)e (K)e-(r)e-(k)o
Henri De Toulouse-Lautrec	An-(r)e (D)e Too-looz Lo-trek
Henri Matisse	An-(r)e Ma-tes
Henri Rousseau	An-(r)e Roo-soo
Jan Van-der Heyden	Yan Van (d)ur Hi-(d)en
Jean Edouard Vuillard	Zhan A-(d)war Vue-(y)ar
Joan Miro	Hwan Me-(r)o
Johan Barthold Jongkind	Yo-han Bar-told Yon(k)int
Leonardo da Vinci	La-o-nar-(d)o (d)a Ven-che
Maurice de Valminck	Mo-(r)es (d)e Vla-mank
Maurice Utrillo	Mo(r)es Oo-tre-lo
Michelangelo Buonanrroti	Mi-(k)el-an-je-lo Bwo-na-(rr)o-ti
Odilon Redon	O-(d)i-lon Re-(d)on
Pablo Picasso	Pablo Pe-(k)-so
Piet Mondrian	Pet Mon-(d)re-an
Rojier Van Der Weyden	Ro-jer-Van (D)er-vi-(d)en
Sanzio Raphael	San-ti-(d)-urbino - (also called)
Theodore Rousseau	The-o-(d)or Roo-soo
Van Rijn Rembrandt	Van-(r)in Rem-brandt (Paul Harmens)
Wassily Kandinsky	Vas-i-le Kan-(d)in-ske
Willem DeKooning	Vil-em De-(k)oo-ning

Famous Orange Physical Athletes

Basketball:

A(d)rian Dantley
An(d)rew Toney
A(k)eem Olajuwon
By(r)on Scott
Cly(d)e Frazier
Domin(q)ue Wil(k)ins - q sounds to k
Earl Mon(r)oe
E(r)ic Floy(d)
Gail Good(r)ich
George Mi(k)an
Jac(k) Si(k)ma
Je(rr)y Lu(c)as - c sounds to k
Je(rr)y West
John Lu(c)as - c sounds to k
Karl Mon(r)oe
Ka(r)eem Ab(d)ul Jabbar
Ki(k)i Van(d)eweghe
La(rr)y Bir(d)
Lenny Wil(k)ins
Mar(k) Agui(rr)e
Mar(k) Jac(k)son
Mi(c)hael Cooper - c sounds to k
Mi(c)hael Jor(d)an - c sounds to k
Mau(r)ice Chee(k)s
Os(c)ar Robertson - c sounds to k
Ric(k) Ba(rr)y
Si(d)ney Mon(c)rief - c sounds to k
Te(rr)y Cummings
Wayman Tils(d)ale
Xavier Mc(d)aniels

Baseball:

An(d)rae Dawson
Billy Will(ia)ms - ia sounds to y
Cal Rip(k)en
Can(d)y Mal(d)anal(d)o
Carl Yastrzems(k)i
Chuc(k) Klein
Da(rr)ell Evans
Da(rr)ell Strawbe(rr)y
Dic(k) Stuart
Du(k)e Sni(d)er
E(dd)ie Mathews
E(dd)ie Mu(rr)y
E(r)ic Davis
Ernie Ban(k)s
Fre(d) Lynn
Fran(k) Howard
Fran(k) Robinson
Fre(d) Will(ia)ms - ia sounds to y
Hac(k) Wilson
Hal Tros(k)y
Han(k) Greenberg
Hen(r)y (Han(k) Aa(r)on
Jac(k) Clar(k)
Jac(k)ie Robinson
Jeff Bu(rr)oughs
Joe (D)iMaggio
Jose Canse(c)o - c sounds to k
Lou Geh(r)ig
Mar(k) McGwire
Mic(k)ey Mantle
Mi(k)e Schmi(d)t
Orlan(d)o Cepa(d)a
Pa(d)ro Gue(rr)e(r)o
Pete In(c)avialgia - c sounds to k

Ric(k)ey Hen(d)erson
Ri(c)o Petrocelli - c sounds to k
Roc(k)y Colavito
Ro(d) Ca(r)ew
Roger Ma(r)is
Te(d) Kluszens(k)i
Te(d) Will(ia)ms - ia sounds to y
Tony Pe(r)ez
Ty(r)us Cobb
Will (Will(ia)m) Clar(k) - ia sounds to y
Willie (Will(ia)m) Mc(K)ovey - ia sounds to y

To help prove my point about the orange creative physical baseball
players let me list some facts for the 1988 baseball season.

At the end of the regular season in the three most important hitting departments: batting average, runs batted in, and home runs - orange physical
players placed as such:

In batting average in the American League the three top hitters were
physical orange people:
1. Wa(d)e Boggs   - .366 pct.
2. Herbie Puc(k)ett   - .356 pct.
3. Mi(k)e Greenwell   - .325 pct.

The three top in RBI's (runs batted in) were all orange physical people:
1. Jose Canse(c)o - (c) sounds to k   - 124 RBIs
2. Herbie Puc(k)ett   - 121 RBIs
3. Mi(k)e Greenwell   - 119 RBIs

The top five in homeruns were all orange-physical people:
1. Jose Canse(c)o - (c) sounds to k   - 42 HR
2. Fre(d) McGriff   - 34 HR
3. Mar(k) McGwire   - 32 HR
4. Ga(r)y Gaetti   - 28 HR
5. Ed(d)ie Mur(r)y   - 28 HR

In the National League, in batting average, four out of the top five were orange physical people:

1. Tony Gwynn — .313 pct.
2. Rafaelo Palmei(r)o — .307 pct.
3. An(d)re Dawson — .303 pct.
4. An(d)res Gala(rr)aga — .302 pct.
5. Ge(r)ald Per(r)y — .300 pct.

In runs batted in (RBIs) five out of the top six are orange physical people:

1. Will [Will(ia)m Clar(k)] - (ia) sounds to y -109 RBIs
2. Da(rr)ell Strawbe(rr)y -101 RBIs
3. Bobby Boni(ll)a - (ll) sounds to y -100 RBIs
4. An(d)y Vansly(k)e -100 RBIs
5. Glenn Davis - 99 RBIs
6. Kevin Mc(R)eynolds - 99 RBIs

There is a possibility that Glenn Davis is also an orange physical person, but because he has no dramatic syllable break in his first name, his name sounds to Glenn - (D)avis. There is a dramatic sound that falls on the (D). If this is true, than all of the leaders I listed in the RBI department would be orange physical people.

In the homerun department, four out of five (or five out of five; depending on Glenn Davis again) came out on top.

1. Da(rr)ell Strawb(rr)y - 39 HR
2. Glenn (D)avis - 30 HR
3. Will [Will(ia)m] Clar(k) - (ia) sounds to y - 29 HR
4. An(d)res Gala(rr)aga - 29 HR
5. Kevin Mc(R)eynolds - 27 HR

Out of the twenty-seven players listed in these departments twenty-four are orange physical people. If we count Glenn Davis as an orange physical person then it would be twenty-six out of twenty-seven, a very stunning percentage.

Now there was and are other great hitters that are not orange physical people, such as (Ba(b)e Ruth, Jimmie Foxx, Harmon Killa (b)rew, Johnny Bench, Dave Kingman, Willie Stargell, Ralph Kiner, George Foster, Richie Allen, Wally Post, Ro(b)erto Clemente, Gorman Thomas, George Bell, Gil Hodges, Dale Murphy, Tony Armas, Al Rosen, Rogers Horns(b)y, Mel Ott, Willie Mays, etc. and I have a few theories on why they were great hitters. In one case, it has to do with the violet letters ("B," "I," "P," "W") trait of "power" as listed in the violet chapter. Another philosophy is that some of these men were either so large or built so strong and stocky that regardless of their letters, when they made good contact with the baseball it was going out of the ballpark, period!

I have other philosophies on sports figures and their talents, but I will withhold them at this time, for I wish not to spend too much time on any one field. In the very near future any formulas or facts that I haven't included or that I'm presently working on, will be discussed in a second book or during speaking engagements.

Why didn't I list any famous orange physical women in my examples? This was done to prove a few points and to ask more questions. First, let me start by stating that a majority of women I interviewed stated that they hated orange! But most said that they did like the light peach-colored oranges. Why is this? Well, my reasoning at this point is: Throughout most of history women have been told by society that certain roles for them were acceptable and others were not. Certain professions were ok, others not; a few being those professions that I used as examples. Look again at some of the orange traits such as self-assurance, venturesome, speculative, exhibitionism, flamboyance. Are these some of the traits which society told women "No-no" to a large degree? I personally disagree with these restricting rules. Women should choose the profession of their choice. Let me also add that I hope that whatever traits women choose to cultivate would be of a kind, creative and positive spiritual nature versus the negative, just like I would anyone else. Let me list some orange physical women in the artistic and sports fields:

Alexan(d)ra Exter - artist

Angeli(c)a Kauffman - (c) sounds to k - artist

Au(d)rey Fla(ck) - artist

Ca(r)ol Mothner - artist

Elizabeth (Sid(d)all -artist

Flo(r)ine Stettheiner - artist

Fri(d)a Kahlo - artist

Georgia O'(K)eefe - artist

Gertrude E(d)erle - swimming

I(r)ene Rice Perei(r)a - artist

Jennifer Du(rr)ant - artist

Joelynn Duesber(r)y -artist

Ju(d)ith Leyster - artist

Ju(d)y Chi(c)ago, (c) sounds to k - artist

Ju(d)y Pfaff - artist

Lavin(ia) Fontana (ia) sounds to y - artist

Ma(r)y Cassatt - artist

Ma(r)ia Sib(y)lla Me(r)ian - artist

Mil(d)red Di(d)(r)ikson - golf and track

Mi(r)iam Schapi(r)o - artist

Patricia Toba(cc)o For(r)ester - (cc) sounds to k - artist

Reme(d)ios Va(r)o - artist

Rosalba Ca(r)(r)ie(r)a - artist

Sa(r)ah Mi(r)iam Peale - artist

Son(ia) Delaunay, (ia) pronounced as y - artist

Son(j)a Henie, (j) sounds to y - figure skater

Sophie An(d)erson - artist

Tama(r)a (d)e Lempi(ck)a - artist

Tama(r)a Press - shot put, discus

Te(r)esa (d)el Pol - artist

Why is it that the majority of very talented female artists are not household names, such as Picasso, Monet, Van Gogh? I have seen the paintings of these women and I am very impressed; in fact, I think they are marvelous artists. Again, I will blame the roles that society tends to put on different groups. I truly hope that female artists will be exposed on a greater level for the pleasure will be to those who view them! Let me also add, that the stories behind many women artists are fascinating!

I would like to add that one can still be physically creative, even though a person may not have any orange physical letters in one's name. One can have orange creative traits in any center and with a little more effort and patience can use other creative centers to transfer them into a physical creative form. You can use your daily creative forces this way also. But the fact does remain that creative orange physical people are naturals at it. If a person happens to be an emotional orange person, it will come very naturally to this person to be creative emotionally and will have a knack of being very creative with others emotionally, and the spiritual orange person will be spiritually creative, and so on, with the other orange center people. Orange people, especially orange physical people, have to be very careful when their spirit is negative because their physical creativeness can easily become a physically destructive trait. Many of the orange physical people I've talked to admitted when they are in a bad mood they tend to throw or break objects. Wherever your creativeness and kindness is centered, culti-vate it and show the world your creative talent.

Let me list some female artists who are not orange physical people, but still used other orange centers or other color traits to transfer these traits into a physical creation:
Alice Neel (emotional orange person)
Be(r)the Mo(r)isot (control orange person)
Jane Wilson (emotional orange person)
Janet Fish (emotional orange person)
(K)ay Sage (spiritual orange person)
Nell Blaine (emotional orange person)
Susan (D)unlap (spiritual orange person)

A person can be in a blue emotional mood and paint a very soulful emotional, blue scenic painting, or create a piece of sculpture with very relaxed soulful lines and features.

A person could be in a yellow spiritual mood and transfer the cheerful yellow traits onto canvas or sculpture, etc.

A person could be in a green physical mood and transfer the traits of balance and poise into any art form.

The combinations of ways to use all of your centers and color traits are just about limitless. I will be happy if I convince those who read this book that we do have the seven centers and the different colors do have the traits that I claim they have, and that they affect us in the ways discussed in this book. Also, I would like to acknowledge the possibilities of new additions and new combinations in which to use the formulas in this book! So don't be afraid to challenge or experiment for yourself, and please remember:

Any profession or business needs all of the color traits to certain degrees. You can apply the red traits of compassion or persistence, or the red trait of physical proof to any field. All fields need the yellow traits of logic and analysis. All fields need the openmindedness and faith of the blue spectrum, the creativity of the orange spectrum, the dedication and regality of the violet spectrum, the practicality and organization of the flesh spectrum. The green traits of poise and balance are needed in all fields. So if you are not an orange physical person, this does not mean that you should not go into the field of art or sports, or if you are not a yellow mental person, you should not go into an intellectual field. Just apply your center-color traits to whichever field you go into or are already in, in the ways that those traits can be used to benefit that particular field. I will give more examples of uses of talent traits for daily use in Chapter Nine.

Sayings That Stimulate Orange Traits

A person who does not construct in work or kindness, destructs, or does nothing at all. Take your pick between the three. - D. G. Rolliet

The drying up a single tear, has more of honest fame, than the shedding seas of gore. - Byron

To cultivate kindness is a valuable part of the business of life. - Johnson

Make a rule, and pray to God to help you to keep it, never, if possible, to lie down at night without being able to say: "I have made one human being at least a little wiser, or a little happier, or at least a little better this day". - Charles Kingsley

A word of kindness is seldom spoken in vain, while witty sayings are as easily lost as the pearls slipping from a broken string. - G. D. Prentice

*Kindness in women, not their beauteous looks shall win my love.
- Shakespeare*

*Sow good services; sweet remembrances will grow from them.
- Madame de Staël*

Jesus and Socrates, out of very different backgrounds, are saying the same thing. Intelligence is kindness. Kindness is intelligence. The fundamental, which the two terms suggest in different ways . . .is the same quality on which all human civilization is built. - Alexander Meiklejohn

I expect to pass through life but once. If therefore, there be any kindness I can show, or any good thing I can do to any fellow- being, let me do it now, and not defer or neglect it, as I shall not pass this way again. - Penn

I have sped much by land, and sea, and mingled with much people, but never yet could find a spot unsunned by human kindness. - Tupper

*Kindness is the golden chain by which society is bound together.
- Goethe*

Kindness is a language the dumb can speak, and the deaf can hear and understand. - Bovee

When death, the great reconciler, has come, it is never our tenderness that we repent of, but our severity. - George Eliot

*What do we live for, if it is not to make life less difficult to each other?
- George Eliot*

*The true and noble way to kill a foe, is not to kill him; you, with kindness, may so change him that he shall cease to be a foe, and then he's slain.
- Aleyn*

Ask thyself, daily, to how many ill-minded persons thou hast shown a kind disposition. - Marcus Antoninus

He that will not give some portion of his ease, his blood, his wealth, for others' good, is a poor, frozen churl. - Joanna Baillie

Both man and womankind-belie their nature when they are not kind. - G. Bailey

Kind words produce their own image in men's souls; and a beautiful image it is. They soothe and quiet and comfort the hearer. They shame him out of his sour, morose, unkind feelings. We have not yet begun to use kind words in such abundance as they ought to be used. - Pascal

Kindness in ourselves is the honey that blunts the sting of unkindness in another. - Landor

Yellow Spectrum
Science - Education - Cheerfulness

The yellow spectrum letters are "E," "L," "S," and "Z". The yellow spectrum ranges from light-tinted yellows to true hue yellows to very dark earthy yellows. Yellow is the intellectual, analytical color; the positive thinking color, the color of cheerfulness and optimism. Other yellow spectrum characteristics: glorification (of God), logic, comprehension, decisiveness, clarity, reasonableness, positiveness, analysis. Yellow is truly the mental color. Yellow mental people are very quick thinkers, they learn quickly, they are usually very logical. Spiritual yellow people are believers of positive thinking; they believe in staying happy and cheerful and to look on the positive side of all situations. The one trait that irritates yellow spiritual people is pessimism. Yellow physical people are physically quick. Yellow people must learn not to move too fast in certain situations. Here are the negative traits to the yellow spectrum which yellow people must guard against: shrewdness, deception, vindictiveness, and pessimism. Yellow spiritual people will have a very hard time if too many unhappy situation occur in their life. So stay positive and stay happy. Yellow people excel in scientific, educational and professional fields or fields where there is the need for mental grasp, and logic, friendliness and cheerfulness. I will also discuss in the blue chapter how yellow traits support the blue traits of imagination are a basic requirement for genius.

Famous people who have cultivated their yellow traits. Notice most scientists and educators are yellow mental people. (Notice many "I's" and "Y's" sound to "E"):

A(l)b(e)rt Ein(s)tein

A(l)(e)xand(e)r Graham B(e)(l)(l)

A(l)(e)xand(e)r Hami(l)ton

A(l)fr(e)d Nob(e)(l)

B(e)njamin Frank(l)in

Char(l)(e)(s) (L)indb(e)rgh

C(l)are Booth

Danie(l) W(e)b(s)t(e)r

D(e)nni(s) Day

(E)ddi(e) A(l)b(e)rt

(E)(l)i Whitn(ey)

(E)(l)ihu Ya(le)

(E)(l)i(z)ab(e)th Tay(l)or

H(e)(l)(e)n Hay(e)(s)

H(e)(l)(e)n K(e)(l)(l)(e)r

H(e)nr(y) Ford

H(e)nr(y) Hud(s)on

H(e)nry (S)tan(l)(e)(y) - y sounds to e

I(s)aac N(e)wton

(L)awr(e)nc(e) W(e)(l)k

(L)(e)(l)and (S)tanford

(L)(e)onardo da Vinc(i) - i sounds to e

(L)i(z)a Min(e)(l)(l)(i) - i sounds to e

(L)uci(l)(l)(e) Ba(l)(l)

Noah W(e)b(s)t(e)r

Phy(l)(l)i(s) Di(l)(l)(e)r

P(i)erre Curri(e) - i sounds to e

P(l)ato

P(l)(i)n(y) - i and y sounds to e

(S)amm(y) Davi(s), Jr. - y sounds to e

(S)ara B(e)rnhardt

(S)a(l)(l)(y) Fi(e)(l)d(s)

(S)hir(l)(e)(y) Mac(L)aine

(S)ocrat(e)(s)
(S)u(z)anne P(l)(e)(s)h(e)tte
Thoma(s) (E)di(s)on
Thoma(s) J(e)ff(e)r(s)on

Sayings That Stimulate Yellow Traits

What sunshine is to flowers, smiles are to humanity. They are but trifles, to be sure; but, scattered along life's pathway, the good they do is inconceivable.

Be cheerful; do not brood over fond hopes unrealized until a chain is fastened on each thought and wound around the heart. Nature intended you to be the fountain-spring of cheerfulness and social life, and not the monument of despair and melancholy. - A. Helps

Logic and metaphysics make use of more tools than all the rest of the sciences put together, and they do the least work. - Colton

A cheerful temper joined with innocence will make beauty attractive, knowledge delightful, and wit goodnatured. It will lighten sickness, poverty, and affliction; convert ignorance into an amiable simplicity , and render deformity itself agreeable. - Addison

If I can put one touch of a rosy sunset into the life of any man or woman, I shall feel that I have worked with God. - G. MacDonald

Cheerfulness is health; its opposite, melancholy, is disease. - Haliburton

Wondrous is the strength of cheerfulness, and its power of endurance— the cheerful man will do more in the same time, will do it better, will persevere in it longer, than the sad or sullen. - Carlyle

Get into the habit of looking for the silver lining of the cloud, and when you have found it, continue to look at it, rather than at the leaden gray in the middle. It will help you over many hard places. - Willitts

If good people would but make their goodness agreeable, and smile instead of frowning in their virtue, how many would they win to the good cause. - Usher

It was a saying of the ancients, that "truth lies in a well;" and to carry on the metaphor, we may justly say, that logic supplies us with steps whereby we may go down to reach the water. - Watts

Cheerfulness is as natural to the heart of a man in strong health, as color to his cheek; and wherever there is habitual gloom, there must be either bad air, unwholesome food, improperly severe labor, or erring habits of life. - Ruskin

God is glorified, not by our groans but by our thanksgivings; and all good thought and good action claim a natural alliance with good cheer. - E.P. Whipple

Be cheerful always, There is no path but will be easier traveled, no load but will be lighter, no shadow on heart and brain but will lift sooner for a person of determined cheerfulness.

Logic is the art of convincing us of some truth. - Bruyere

Oh, give us the man who sings at his work. - Carlyle

The highest wisdom is continual cheerfulness; such a state, like the region above the moon, is always clear and serene. - Montaigne

You have not fulfilled every duty unless you have fulfilled that of being cheerful and pleasant. - C. Buxton

Green Spectrum
Poise - Balance - Justice

Green spectrum letters are "F," "M," and "T". The green spectrum ranges from light white greens to true hue green to dark forest greens. Green is the color of balance and control (self-control) and poise. The positive traits of the green spectrum are: impartiality (fairness), equitableness (agree-ableness), lawfulness, cooperativeness, critical discrimination, caution, and peacefulness.

The negative traits: bias, disagreeableness, callousness, envy, suspicion, lack of judgement, sense of injustice, miserliness. I also call green the ego color; green people must be careful not to get into ego battles with others. Anyone that upsets a green person's senses of poise or of being "in control" will trigger a threat to a green person's ego balance, and the ego (one-upmanship) battle will start. Green people must guard against playing the macho game to extreme. If a green person (spiritual, mental, vocal, physical, control, emotional or sexual) is truly poised, in control and at peace with one self, one will not let these other people trigger these responses. Green people excel in careers that require poise and balance and control such as models, pro quarterbacks, professional golfers, judges, ballerinas, ecological environment specialists and the field of weight balancing in structures such as bridges, monuments, and large buildings, which is the field of architecture. Green people make very good scientists and inventors, because green is the combination of yellow (intellect) and blue (imagination).

Famous Green People:

Models:

Cheryl (T)iegs - spiritual green person
Chris(t)y Brinkley - dramatic/physical green person
Chris-(t)y (T)urling-(t)on - spiritual, double dramatic/
physical green person
Cindy Craw-(f)ord - dramatic/physical green person
Elle (M)acpherson - spiritual green person
I(m)an - mental and dramatic/physical green person
Jean Shri(m)p-(t)on - control center and dramatic/physical green person
Lauren Hu(t)(t)on - control center and dramatic/physical green person
Sa-(m)an-(t)ha Jones - double dramatic/physical green person
S(t)e(ph)anie Sey(m)our - mental, double dramatic/physical green person
(ph) sounds to (f)
(T)wiggy - spiritual green person
Wilhel-(m)ina - dramatic/physical green person

Quarterbacks:

Bar(t) S(t)arr
Ber(t) Jones
Bob Wa(t)er(f)ield
Boo(m)er Easiason

Craig (M)or(t)on
Dan (F)ou(t)s
Don (M)eride(t)h
Doug (F)lu(t)ie
(F)ran (T)arken(t)on
(F)rankie Alber(t)
George (M)ira
Ji(m) Kelly
Ji(m) (M)c-(M)ahon
Ji(m) Plunke(t)(t)
Joe (M)on(t)ana
Joe Na(m)a(t)h
John Elway - emotional green person
Johnny Uni(t)as
Kenny S(t)abler
Nor(m)an Van Brocklin
O(t)(t)o Graha(m)
(P)hil Si(m)(m)s - p sounds to f
Roger S(t)aubach
Sa(m)(m)y Baugh
S(t)eve Bar(t)kowski
S(t)eve Young
(T)erry Bradshaw
(T)o(m)(m)y Kra(m)er
Warren (M)oon
Y.A. (T)i(t)(t)le

Famous Female Architects:

Ber(t)ha Yerez Whi(t)(m)an
Doris Cole - emotional green person
Edla (M)uir
Eleanor Ray(m)ond
Elizabe(t)h Coi(t)
Elizabe(t)h (M)ar(t)ini
(F)lorence Cusco(m)b
Gabrille Cle(m)en(t)s

Hazel Wood Wa(t)er(m)an
Ida Anna Ryan - emotional green person
Julia (M)organ - San Simeon (Hearst Castle)
Laura Hayes - emotional green person
Lilly Reich - emotional green person
Louise Blanchard Be(t)hune
Louise Howe - emotional green person
Lu(t)ah (M)aria Riggs
(M)arcia (M)ead
(M)argare(t) Hicks
(M)arie (F)ro(m)(m)er
(M)arion (M)ahony Gri(f)(f)in
(M)ary Ho(m)(m)ann
(M)ary O(t)is S(t)evens
(M)inevra Parker
Na(t)alie de Blois
So(p)hia Hayden - p sounds to f
So(p)hie (T)aeuber - p sounds to f
(T)heoda(t)e Pope Riddle

Famous Male Architects:

Ar(t)hur B. (M)ulle(t)
Benja(m)in Henry La(t)robe - U.S. Capitol Building
(F)ilippo Brunelleschi - Florence Cathedral
(F)rank Lloyd Wrigh(t)
Henry Bacon - emotional green person - Lincoln Memorial
Ik(t)inos - Parthenon - Athens
Ja(m)es Hoban - U.S. Capitol
John (F)rancis - Westminister Cathedral
John Por(t)(m)an
Jose(ph) S(t)rauss - (ph) sounds to f - Golden Gate Bridge
Kallikra(t)es - Parthenon - Athens
Louis Chris(t)ian (M)ullgrad(t)
(M)ichelangelo Buonarro(t)i
(M)ike Graves
(M)nesikles - Gateway to the Acropolis

O(t)h(m)an Her(m)an A(m)(m)an - Verrazzano - Narrows Bridge, NY
Rober(t) (M)ills - Washington Monument
(T)ho(m)as Ha(m)il(t)on
(T)ho(m)as Je(f)(f)erson
(T)ho(m)as Wal(t)er - U.S. Capitol
(T).Y. Lin - Famous Bridge Builder
Willia(m) Bu(t)(t)er(f)ield

Green cultivated people usually have very strong bonds with the green
ecology system of trees, forests, and greenery of all plant life. Two classic
examples of this are John (M)uir and Henry David (T)horeau. Both green
spiritual people, the trees and forests had very strong spiritual effects upon
these two men, as we can tell from their incredible efforts to preserve the
natural forests. Green people are usually make very good gardeners and do
very well in fields related to horticulture. One of my life-long-emotional
colors is green, and whenever I go into a forest of trees, or just go out in the
back yard and sit under the green shade of a tree, it has a very relaxing
affect on my emotions.

Green is also a very good healing color. Remember, green is the color of
poise and balance, so it is very restful in this sense; and when we're sick,
one of the first prescribed rules for healing is to rest. We get the majority
of our natural medicines and drugs from green tree leaves and plants,
which pull in free oxygen (fresh air), which is necessary in healing, in a
lot of cases.

Blue Spectrum
Spiritual - Imaginative - Dependable

Blue spectrum color letters are "G," "N," and "U". The blue spectrum
ranges from light white blues to true hue blue to dark night navy blues.
Blue is the spiritual color, the color of faith, the soul color. Blue is the
color of the ethereal, celestial, spiritual world. Here are the traits that fall
under the rays of the blue spectrum: (spirited, faithfulness, dutifulness,
mediative, serenity (sense of beauty), inventiveness (openmindedness),
diplomacy (tactfulness), soulful. On the other hand, the negative traits are

superstition, indiscretion, distrust, apathy, laziness, lack of faith, lack of trust. Blue is soothing and mediative. Blue is the most spiritual of colors, the color of believers in the spiritual world. The greatest spiritual person and the Savior, Jesus - pronounced (G)e-zus, and other spiritual persons such as (G)a(n)dhi (Moha(n)dis Ka(n)amcha(n)o), Joh(n) the Baptist, Marti(n) L(u)ther Ki(ng) J(u)(n)ior, chose to cultivate their blue spiritual traits. Other blue spiritual persons who cultivated these traits in their fields were people such as He(n)ry David Thoreau, Joh(n) M(u)ir, Joha(n)(n) Wolf(g)a(n)(g) (G)oethe, Alfred (N)obel, Rola(n)d T. Hu(n)t (spiritual color analyst), Cori(n)(n)e Heli(n)e (author of Healing and Regeneration through Color) and many more. Blue spiritual people have an incredible amount of faith that problems will eventually work themselves out.

Blue is also what I call the imagination color, the color of genius. Blue is just like a clear blue sky open, spacious, and meditative. If we think about it logically, how does one obtain genius? Well, one is labeled genius when a person discovers or invents something new or incredible that others find even hard to "imagine". Let's look at how one invents or discovers these acts of genius. First, one has to have "faith" that these feats are possible. This is what we call an "open mind" (a main trait of the blue spectrum). You'll probably never find a closed-minded genius. Then, a person must open the mind even farther to search for the different possibilities to answer questions on how to achieve these feats. One needs space and room to explore; if one fails on the first attempt one must look elsewhere, and again and again, until this person finds these answers. But you cannot find the answers if the door is shut in your mind. You must open those different doors. A person has to withstand the pressures and criticisms from other small-minded people by the acts of "soulfulness" and faith. If you check the history books and biographies of most geniuses, you find that most were severely shunned, had their lives threatened or were thrown into jail, called "crazymen", lunatics, liars, enemies of their country and ridiculed by their own teachers, friends and family. But through all this pressure, they still dug very, very deep into their souls to continue to hold on to their beliefs and see them through. These are the first stages of genius.

The second stage comes after a person finds and retains the answers, (which usually comes out of the "blue"), as a gift of faith and hard work for these beliefs. (Take for example Albert Einstein's quote): "I didn't arrive at my understanding of the fundamental laws of the universe through my rational mind." A person must then "logically analyze" (yellow color trait) the findings. Then, after one has determined the logic of ones findings, this person must then "organize" these findings and put them to "practical" use, both flesh color traits. That is when one has completed all of the basic stages of genius. (It also helps to have the dedication of the violet spectrum and the green and red color traits of poise and persistence). There will usually be rough edges to smooth by the inventor himself or others to follow, or the ongoing fact of possible new or better inventions. The wide open "Blue" to explore. The doors of the mind that will need to be opened to the infinite realm of the blue spectrum. One also gets imagination from one's spiritual center traits.

Famous Blue Inventors are:

Albert Ei(n)stei(n)
Alexa(n)der (G)raham Bell
Be(n)jami(n) Fra(n)kli(n)
Eli Whit(n)ey
(G)(u)(g)lielmo Marco(n)i
(G)alileo (G)alilei
He(n)ry Ford
Ire(n)e Joliot C(u)rie
Isaac (N)ewto(n)
Leo(n)ardo da Vi(n)ci
Lo(u)is Paste(u)r
(N)icholas Coper(n)ic(u)s
Pierre C(u)rie
Sam(u)el Fi(n)ley Breese Morse

Blue people are also very soulful, especially blue emotional people. Blue emotional people usually have a very soulful laugh. They relax around blue lakes, blue waters, blue skies and blue interiors. Blue people must guard against being too soulful or too spirited in certain situations. They tend to be too open and spread themselves too thin if they are not careful. They must also guard against being too cold in their feelings.

Blue people also make excellent interior decorators. I recently counted 417 interior designers listed in a directory in a major metropolitan area. Out of those 417 listed, 327 of them had many blue letters in their names. (I accredit this correlation to the (sense of beauty) and (serenity) traits of the blue spectrum.)

Sayings That Stimulate Blue Traits

Faith makes the discords of the present the harmonies of the future. - Collyer

Artists treat facts as stimuli for imagination, whereas scientist use imagination to coordinate facts. - Arthur Koestler

An uncommon degree of imagination constitutes poetical genius. - Dugald Stewart

Either we have an immortal soul or we have not. If we have not, we are beasts; the first and wisest of beasts it may be; but still beasts. We only differ in degree, and not in kind; just as the elephant differs from the slug. But by the concession of the materialists, we are not of the same kind as beasts; and this also we say from our own consciousness. Therefore, me thinks, it must be the possession of a soul within us that makes the difference. - Coleridge

The body, that is but dust; the soul, it is a bud of eternity. - N. Culverwell

Faith makes all evil good to us, and all good better; unbelief makes all good evil, and all evil worse. Faith laughs at the shaking of the spear; unbelief trembles at the shaking of a leaf, unbelief starves the soul; faith finds food in famine, and a table in the wilderness. In the greatest danger, faith says, "I have a great God." When outward strength is broken, faith rests on the promises. In the midst of sorrow, faith draws the sting out of every trouble, and takes out the bitterness from every affliction. - Cecil

Science has sometimes been said to be opposed to faith, and inconsistent with it. — But all science, in fact, rests on a basis of faith, for it assumes the permanence and uniformity of natural laws—a thing which can never be demonstrated. - Tryon Edwards

The human race built most nobly when limitations were greatest and, therefore, when most was required of imagination in order to build at all. Limitations seem to have always been the best friends of architecture. - Frank Lloyd Wright

It is the divine attribute of the imagination, that when the real world is shut out it can create a world for itself, and with a necromantic power can conjure up glorious shapes and forms, and brilliant visions to make solitude populous, and irradiate the gloom of a dungeon.
- Washington Irving

The problem of restoring to the world original and eternal beauty is solved by the redemption of the soul. - Emerson

It seems to me as if not only the form but the soul of man was made to walk erect and look upon the stars. - Bulwer

The steps of faith fall on the seeming void, but find the rock beneath.
- Whittier

The soul without imagination is what an observatory would be without a telescope. - H.W. Beecher

The human soul is like a bird that is born in a cage. Nothing can deprive it of its natural longings, or obliterate the mysterious remembrance of its heritage. - Epes Sargent

To look upon the soul as going on from strength to strength, to consider that she is to shine forever with new eternity; that she will be still adding virtue to virtue, and knowledge to knowledge,- -carries in it something wonderfully agreeable to that ambition which is natural to the mind of man. - Addison

Faith is the root of all good works; a root that produces nothing is dead. - Daniel Wilson

The faculty of imagination is the great spring of human activity, and the principal source of human improvement. As it delights in presenting to the mind scenes and characters more perfect than those which we are acquainted with, it prevents us from ever being completely satisfied with our present condition, or with our past attainments, and engages us continually in the pursuit of some untried enjoyment, or of some ideal excellence. Destroy this faculty, and the condition of man will become as stationary as that of the brutes. - Dugold Stewart

The wealth of a soul is measured by how much it can feel; its poverty by how little. - W.R. Alger

I am fully convinced that the soul is indestructible, and that its activity will continue through eternity. It is like the sun, which, to our eyes, seems to set in night; but it has in reality only gone to diffuse its light elsewhere. - Goethe

To believe is to be strong. Doubt cramps energy. Belief is power. - F.W. Robertson

Imagination disposes of everything; it creates beauty, justice, and happiness, which are everything in this world. - Pascal

Heaven-born, the soul a heavenward course must hold; beyond the world she soars; the wise man, I affirm, can find no rest in that which perishes, nor will he lend his heart to aught that doth on time depend. - Michael Angelo

When men cease to be faithful to their God, he who expects to find them so to each other will be much disappointed. - George Horne

The human mind cannot create anything. It produces nothing until after having been fertilized by experience and meditation; its acquisitions are the germs of its production. - Buffon

Narrow minds think nothing right that is above their own capacity. - Rochefoucauld

The saddest of all failures is that of a soul, with its capabilities and possibilities, failing of life everlasting, and entering on that night of death upon which no morning ever dawns. - Herrick Johnson

There are few who need complain of the narrowness of their minds if they will only do their best with them. - Hobbes

Life is the soul's nursery—its training place for the destinies of eternity. - Thackeray

White

Holiness - Giving - Healing

White is said to be the God light and the Christ light. It is very anti-gravitational, non-earthly, very giving, very purifying, very protective, and very cleansing and healing. To cultivate the characteristics of white is to become very spiritual, to become closer to God, to shed the dark earthly trappings of sin and materialism. White light reflects ninety-eight percent light and consumes two percent, therefore, it allows us to see in its presence. When one wants to uplift one's spirit when one's spirit has become very bad or too earthly, one should visualize and imagine breathing in white light through any of one's seven spiritual energy centers. Interior decorators use white color and color that has been tinted with white to add spirit and brightness and cleanliness to rooms. As I mentioned before, the characteristics of white are protectiveness and cleanliness—just look at the color used mostly in hospitals by doctors and nurses; just imagine if they all wore black! Not very encouraging, right? White is active and positive. Try wearing white after having a spiritual cleansing and see how good it will feel on and around you. White light allows all things to unfold and awaken our higher spiritual selves.

Light is capable of incredible energy. It can illuminate vast areas. Light from the sun can generate electrical energy through solar panels, which can heat, illuminate, our homes, and run all the equipment in them nowadays. This seems to be the energy of the future, for it is clean and safe. What other form of energy can we associate most accepted and blessed by God than solar energy, which does not poison His beloved Mother Earth that He has given us? Do you think He would vote for poisonous fossil fuels or extremely poisonous and dangerous nuclear energy versus clean energy such as solar? There are solar collectors in service nowadays that create heat that is 3,300 degrees Celsius, that direct this light heat energy to a furnace that melts steel 1 cm. thick in less than one minute! Just recently a major university has discovered a way to make solar panels much more effective and a scientist from India has made a very thin lightweight solar cell that some claim will reduce the cost of solar installation from approximately $25,000 to $5,000. What about the incredible power of laser light beams? So, as we can see, light and colors can play very important roles in our lives now and in the future.

Those that have cultivated the traits of the white spectrum are very giving, wholesome, religious and very good healers, and do very well in fields that need these qualities.

Gray
Neutrality - Mutual Agreement - Separator

The gray spectrum ranges from light silver grays to very dark ash grays. Gray is achieved by the mixture of white and black. White (spiritual and giving), black (consuming and earthy). Gray is the color of neutrality, neither aggressive nor backing up, gray stands it's neutral ground. Gray is mutual agreement (giving and taking). Gray is like a prism or mist from rain which allows the colors of the rainbows to be reflected or be exposed.

Therefore gray has the natural ability to separate the contents of elements into their true hues or character. Those people who have all seven of the color letters in their name will be gray emotional people, so gray emotional people will take on the characteristics which I have just mentioned. They will be neutral emotionally; not wanting to take sides in most matters. They give back that which is given to them in equal return, and they have a natural ability to expose and separate the facts into their particular categories. If you compliment gray emotional people, they will compliment you. If you help them, they will help you. If you don't, they won't. If you're kind to them, they'll be kind to you. Gray people are like a mirror; they reflect back just what they see. If one wants to tone down other colors, if they feel those colors are too bright, too bold or strong, one should mix gray with them to mellow them down, and render them a little bit more neutral. Gray has a relaxing effect when one has to tone down the emotions, or if one has the habit of becoming overly involved in too many emotional situations. Gray emotional persons tend to relax on gray overcast or foggy days.

Gray people make good diplomats, judges, negotiators, and excel in careers where there is a need to limit strong emotions.

Sayings That Stimulate Gray Traits

Giving and taking the mutual agreement that makes marriage a delight. - D.G. Rolliet

When in the act of investigating, make sure first to divorce your prejudices from the investigation in order to get the accurate facts, then fair judgement can be made. - D.G. Rolliet

Black
Rest - Consuming - New Beginnings

The characteristics of black are very consuming - it consumes ninety-eight percent light while reflecting two percent. Black is secretive (hidden). These two traits are the reason why many consider black to be very seductive and sexy, because of its ability to draw in, in a consuming and discreet way. Black is firm-in-opinion (serious commitment) and it is also anger when in a negative black mood. Priest choose black for their habits as a firm commitment to God and celibacy. Black is new beginnings, the ending of ways of doing things in one way, and the commitment to do things in a different way! This is the mood we are in when we say to ourselves or others "I'm not doing that any more - that's it!" Sound familiar? Black is very gravitational. It draws in. God gave us the darkness of night in which to rest and regenerate our energy so that when the light of day (dawn) comes, we will be rested, to use our energy for the use of activity in the light of day. We should use black when we want to listen and consume and rest. Whenever I want someone to listen to what I have to say, I ask them to think of the color black in a quiet consuming way, this way they absorb more of what I have to say! Try this with others or yourself. These are some of the different moods you will be in when you choose black for use. The negative traits of black are: trappings of dark earthy sin, anti-spiritual and anti-God, excessive anger.

7
Favorite Colors

7

Favorite Colors

I have found, through thousands of interviews, that a person's favorite colors over a long period of time will be the colors that correspond to the energy centers that they have cultivated the most. For example if a person has cultivated their mental center, then that persons life-long mental color will be one of that persons favorite colors. If a person has cultivated one's control center, then that life-long control color will be a favorite color. If a person has cultivated one's emotional and sexual centers, then the favorites will be one's life-long emotional-sexual colors. If a person starts to cultivate new centers, one will start to accept and like these new center-colors. I have also found that when a person dislikes a color, it is usually because this person has not cultivated this center very much or has had a very negative experience pertaining to that particular center. For example, if a person dislikes one's emotional center color there is a good chance this person has had one or many negative emotional experiences, such as many broken, or very negative emotional love-mate experiences. Another reason which could "turn-off" a person to a color would be a very traumatic experience in or around a certain color, such as a person being robbed and mugged in a very frightful way by a person wearing a certain red shirt, causing a bad association experience with that certain color of red.

As I mentioned earlier, overall, women's favorite colors were their emotional-center colors. I am presently involved in further studies of this nature and especially studies on the favorite colors of men.

We also have had social color associations such as some consider red as danger, black as evil, yellow as cowardice, etc. Most of these associations being negative and immature in nature, which cause a bad "mind set" against these colors. This book is meant to be much more detailed and analytical and personal than those general social associations.

8
Your Daily Colors

8
Your Daily Colors

Our daily colors reflect our daily moods in our seven centers. As I have discussed, our general personality moods and characteristic traits are revealed through our name, but we are not always in the life-long moods. We tend to change moods every day or two. If a certain subject question or points of view are asked of us, we usually fall back into our life-long points of view on these questions or situations, and in the way we've formed our opinions. For example; if your life-long spiritual color is blue, you will always look somewhat youthful and wholesome in blue and usually hold to your blue spiritual philosophies. But as you will find out by reading this chapter that blue on some days may be your daily-control-center color, or it could be your daily emotional-center color, and so on, with your other centers. In the case of it being your daily control-color, then you would predominately look very controlled and regal in blue and you would also look somewhat youthful because of your youthful life-long association with blue. If, in the case blue happened to be your daily emotional center color, you would mostly look relaxed and romantic in blue and, to a certain degree, youthful in it again retaining that life-long association. This general formula stands true for all your seven life-long colors.

Your daily center colors will appear the most accurate to the center traits that they are attuned to because your daily colors and traits will be exactly how you feel and project on a daily basis. It's kind of like this. If your favorite life-long food happens to be pizza, but today you are "just craving" enchiladas, then enchiladas will taste the best to you, right? So this chapter is devoted to our daily moods and colors which will help us on a daily basis, to tune into ourselves for use in our daily wardrobe situations, for job interviews, special events, auditions, pleasing love mates, and relaxing. The first step to get into tune with your seven centers and colors is, upon rising every morning, take your color fan (which I've included in this book). True hue red, orange, yellow, green, blue, violet, and flesh fan, containing the seven colors in their true hue, and eight other cards which include the full scale of these seven colors from their light tints to dark shades and one card for the gray spectrum which ranges from light gray to dark ash gray, plus white and black (and other color mixture cards which I will explain later in this chapter). Go to a good source of natural light (such as a window or an open door) and spread out your seven true hue colors and their tints and shades.

The second step is (while in a good source of light) to put the true hue card with the seven true hue colors, red, orange, yellow, green, blue, violet, and flesh up against your face and look into a mirror. Now you're ready to start to tune into your seven centers. I start by finding what I consider are my three easiest colors to get in tune with, and those are my spiritual, physical, and mental. Once you find these three, you will automatically know your other four color centers because your sexual will be the opposite of your spiritual, your emotional, the opposite of your physical, and your control, the opposite of your mental. Then the only center left will be your vocal. Here is my center-opposite chart and my color-opposite chart.

Centers
Spiritual - Sexual
Physical - Emotional
Mental - Control
Vocal

Colors
red - green
orange - blue
yellow - violet
flesh - gray

So, let's start with your spiritual color. Put the seven true hue colors up against your face and see which one of those colors looks and feels the most youthful, clean, wholesome and cheerful against your skin while smiling (smiling is a youthful, wholesome, cheerful trait). I also say those words aloud or to myself as I do this, because you're not only trying to find your spiritual color, but the traits that make you feel this way. For example; if you were to find that red was your spiritual color this day, then the romantic traits of the red color will also make you feel youthful and clean. Once you find your spiritual color, you will then know your sexual color by using the opposite charts. Let's say again, if red happens to be your spiritual, then green would be your sexual, If red were your spiritual color, then go to the full spectrum scale card on your fan of this color. Say the words again to yourself, youthful, clean, cheerful to find out exactly where you're at in that color spectrum. Are you in a light-pink spiritual mood or a dark red spiritual mood? Do the same with your sexual color using words like sexy, seductive, and sultry. Let's move on to your physical center color, again putting the remaining colors against your face while saying the words, "physical, dramatic, physical work color, and compassionate," and seeing which one of the remaining colors has this effect. Your physical color will contrast and look the most dramatic against your skin. It will also look the most physically masculine and boldly warm and truthful, so using these words and feelings, you'll be able to find your physical color. Then, using the opposite charts, you'll find your emotional color. If green happens to be your daily dramatic color, then red would be your emotional color. Then, find out exactly where, in those spectrums, you stand physically and emotionally. The words to use in your emotional color will be feminine, emotional, gentle, relaxed, romantic. Your emotional color will blend the smoothest with your skin. It will have the least contrast.

The next color center to get in tune with is your mental center color. This color will look very practical, simple (non-flashy), logical, and intellectual. Just say these words, and use your feedback while viewing the remaining colors to find your mental color. Once you have found your mental-center color you will then know your control-center color, which is the opposite of your mental-center color. Just check the opposite chart.

Your control color will look very regal/royal, stately, refined/cultured and powerful. Now you have six of your colors, and the remaining color will be your vocal color, which will look fluent, vibrant, clean in tone (conversational) and the other traits I mentioned in the life-long vocal center chapter. If you have problems finding your colors by using the color fan let me suggest a way that I have personally found you can use, along with your fan-skin-feedback method of finding your colors. I have collected pictures of rooms that are decorated in each of the seven colors plus a gray room from decorating magazines. Rooms decorated in one color are quite common in these magazines, so you shouldn't have to look very hard to find them. Start by looking through any old or current magazines you have laying around and ask friends and relatives for their old magazines. Take these pictures and put them in a folder or pin them to a cork board. Using basically the same feedback method as the color fan, study these different room colors while imagining yourself in these rooms, one at a time. Start again with your spiritual. Ask yourself what room feels clean, fresh and spiritual. Then, go to your mental room color and so on. After you find all your center colors, go back to your fan and find out exactly where you are at in those colors. Light green or dark green? Light blue or dark blue? by using your tint and shades color cards. I strongly suggest using this room colors method, for I find it works very well. The main reason it works well is because, when you imagine yourself in these rooms, you're surrounding yourself with the whole color in effect.

One other way of finding your colors is simply go to your closet and try on the different colors. By feel and look, determine which one feels youthful, which one feels and looks dramatic. Do the rest of your colors this way. This method also works very well.

Remember: Besides looking in a visual way for your center-colors, you are also searching for the feeling traits of your center- colors. For example; If you're looking for your spiritual center- color and you are undecided between blue and yellow, go to the color chapters that explain the different traits of these two colors and ask yourself, "Does the imaginative and soul traits of the blue spectrum make me feel youthful and wholesome, etc., or does the logical and analytical traits of the yellow spectrum make me feel youthful-spirited-wholesome, etc.

I have also included other color mixtures such as *green-blue, yellow-green, violet-red, violet-blue, red-orange, yellow-orange,* for days when you find yourself going through mood changes and you find yourself in these combination color moods. There will be many days when you will not be in pure color moods, such as pure red or pure blue. Days when you find that your center colors are in a color combination such as: red-orange, then your opposite center color will be green-blue. Here are the color combination opposite formulas:

red-orange/green-blue
yellow-orange/violet-blue
yellow-green/violet-red
flesh mixed with any color - grey mixed with the opposite color of the color mixed with flesh - this color combination seldom occurs.

Daily Center-Color Photographs

The following photographs will show all the models wearing two of their daily center-colors. Most of the models are wearing solid colors. I used solid colors for different reasons. First, it shows visually very well the effects of the models daily center-color traits; and secondly, solid colors were the most available colors in the stores where I shopped for the outfits. I analyzed each model's colors approximately 3 to 4 hours before each photo shooting session. I would then go directly to a nearby shopping mall that had several stores in which to find the models' daily colors and their correct sizes as close to what was available. I was limited also to certain styles, textures and sheens of the garments that were available at the stores mainly because of seasonal styles that were offered by the stores at this time. After finding and purchasing these garments I would proceed directly to the photographers studio for a prearranged shooting time. Even though there were these limiting factors involved, the following photos will show the rewarding positive visual effects of tuning an individual into one's daily colors.

I would like to also add that in the near future I have plans of opening stores that will stock a very large selection of colors, styles, sheens, prints and sizes that will supply the needs of individuals and businesses for special functions such as gala events, weddings, beauty contests, romantic encounters, commercials, advertisements, (video and print) auditions, interviews and photographic sessions. For inquiries about these services you can write "Color Diplomats" at P.O. Box 21, Crockett, CA. 94525, or call 415-787-1810. Life-long consulting for wardrobe, home-decor, business and natural center talent traits for analyzing career choices is also available.

RELAXED and ROMANTIC
Heidi wearing her daily Emotional-Center Color

DRAMATIC and AGGRESSIVE
Heidi wearing her daily Physical-Center Color

REFINED and REGAL

Bill wearing his daily Control-Center Color

DRAMATIC and AGGRESSIVE

Bill wearing his daily Physical-Center Color

YOUTHFUL and WHOLESOME
Irene wearing her daily Spiritual-Center Color

SEXY and SEDUCTIVE
Irene wearing her daily Sexual-Center Color

INTELLECTUAL and PRACTICAL
Sheila wearing her daily Mental-Center Color

REFINED and REGAL
Sheila wearing her daily Control-Center Color

YOUTHFUL and WHOLESOME
Margaret wearing her daily Spiritual-Center Color

RELAXED and ROMANTIC
Margaret wearing her daily Emotional-Center Color

YOUTHFUL and WHOLESOME
Carolyn wearing her daily Spiritual-Center Color

SEXY and SEDUCTIVE
Carolyn wearing her daily Sexual-Center Color

DRAMATIC and AGGRESSIVE
Augie wearing his daily Physical-Center Color

RELAXED and ROMANTIC
Augie wearing his daily Emotional-Center Color

	1	2	3	4	5	6	7	
TRUE HUES	1	2	3	4	5	6	7	◯
YELLOW	8	9	10	11	12	13	14	◯
YELLOW ORANGE	15	16	17	18	19	20	21	◯
ORANGE	22	23	24	25	26	27	28	◯
RED ORANGE	29	30	31	32	33	34	35	◯
RED	36	37	38	39	40	41	42	◯
VIOLET RED	43	44	45	46	47	48	49	◯
VIOLET	50	51	52	53	54	55	56	◯
VIOLET BLUE	57	58	59	60	61	62	63	◯
BLUE	64	65	66	67	68	69	70	◯
GREEN BLUE	71	72	73	74	75	76	77	◯
GREEN	78	79	80	81	82	83	84	◯
YELLOW GREEN	85	86	87	88	89	90	91	◯
FLESH	92	93	94	95	96	97	98	◯
WHITE GRAY BLACK	99	100	101	102	103	104		◯

PASTE THIS PAGE TO CARD-WEIGHT PAPER, AND CUT BETWEEN COLORS AND ASSEMBLE AT HOLES

Shopping for Daily Center-Color Garments for Special Occasions

Here are a few different methods I use to shop for daily center- color garments.

1. Rise early and analyze your colors and decide which center- color you want to wear for your special occasion.

2. Leave as early as possible for a large store or large shopping mall, or an area where there is a large selection of stores in which you can have a greater chance of finding your color in your size and style that is right for your occasion. Make sure you bring your color-fan with you. You should do this for two important reasons. First, it is very hard to remember and match a specific color just on memory. The second reason being, if you can't find your first center-color choice, then you should pick one of your other daily center-colors because any one of them will look very good on you. So don't worry if you can't find your main choice. If you can't shop for your daily center-colors on a special occasion day, you can wear your life-long center-color of the center you are trying to project. For example, if red is your daily control color and you can't find or shop for this red, then wear your life-long control color. You will always look somewhat controlled in your life-long control color, and it will become somewhat natural for you to project the traits and feelings of your life-long traits, and you can shop and prepare your outfit days or weeks in advance. If you can't find any of your colors, you should pick between white, gray, or black. Pick white if most of your daily colors are in the light end of the spectrums, because those colors are all mixed with white, so white will look very good on you. If most of your colors on this day are medium true hue colors, such as medium blue or medium true red, etc., then go to gray and it will look very well on you. If most of your colors are in the dark end of the spectrum, then go to black. There are some occasions and functions when wearing white, gray, black or other colors will not be appropriate, so before you wear any color to a special occasion if you don't know whether this color is acceptable, then ask someone "in the know."

3. If you are pressed for time, cut up as many pieces of your colors as possible and go to several stores. Drop off the swatches of colors to the sales staff and ask them to look for those colors in your size and style and tell them you will return. This way you have several people looking at once. I would also advise taking along a friend; this way you can split up and cover more stores in a shorter time.

Sewing for Daily Special Occasions

For those of you that sew, you can begin preparing for your special occasion by making a sample garment several days or weeks in advance out of muslin or some other material that you feel will drape in the style that you've picked for your garment. Then on the day of your special occasion, rise early, read your colors, and proceed to a fabric store that stocks a very large selection of fabric colors, purchase your fabric, return home and sew your garment (make sure you have your pattern with final fitting adjustments made all cut out and laid out ready to go). If you don't sew, you can arrange with a seamstress to make the garment for you.

If you can't shop or sew for your special occasion garments you can write or call to check if I have a store or shopping service coming to your area.

9

Use of Daily Colors in Relationships

9

Use of Daily Colors in Relationships

The use of your daily color traits can be used on a daily basis in relation-ships. An excellent way to enrich your daily life, and that of others, is by using the daily color system which I explained in Chapter 8. Use this system on anyone you wish, to interact in whatever type of relationship, to promote better understanding of one another. You can use your daily colors to stimulate yourself or others spiritually, mentally, vocally, physi-cally, self-control, emotionally or sexually. We've all experienced the maximum effect of feelings of different aspects of life. For example, the wonderful taste of delicious food after being hungry for several hours. It seems as if the food just melts in our mouth. We've all experienced the wonderful feeling of a nice hot bath after a long hard day of hard, dirty work! Or after several days of stress or depression, and we have a wonder-ful soulful belly laugh that just washes away all that stress and worry instantly. Or, how about those days when we get a good night's sleep and wake up feeling fresh and clean and youthful on a beautiful clear spring-like day; or a nice hug from a loved one when we're feeling bad; or a wonderful compliment out of the clear blue when we don't expect it. These are what I call maximum effect feelings that affect our different centers through our different senses. By way of tuning into your daily center color mood traits, you can learn to have more of these wonderful maximum feelings that just send shivers down your spine. For example, if a wife wants to stimulate her husband sexually, she should find out what his daily sexual color is, wear that color, and act out the character traits of that color, then have her husband wear and project her daily sexual mood color in return. They'll have a very good chance of achieving one of those maximum effect feelings! If you want to relax and communicate with your love mate on an emotional level, find out their emotional center color, wear that color, and project the traits of that color. If a person happens to be trying to make a sale on a product or a service, the most important selling point is how this product or service will benefit the buyer. I would advise the seller to wear their daily mental color to project their practical mental thoughts to the buyer.

Note: You can use life-long center colors to stimulate whatever traits you wish in yourself or others.

We not only have relations with other people, but with our jobs, careers, talents and decisions. Here are some examples of how to use your daily color traits.

Note: Before doing any of the suggested physical exercises consult your physician.

Flesh

Days when you are in a flesh spiritual mood are good days for being open, imaginative, and happy about music, organizing and behaving morally.

Days when you are in a flesh mental mood are good days to organize in a very practical way and for analyzing your musical ideas, also good for being frugal and organizing your finances.

Days when you are in a flesh vocal mood are good days for harmonizing your voice and singing.

Days when you are in a flesh physical mood are good days to work on your coordination, and also operatic singing from deep in your lungs.

Days when you are in a flesh control mood are good days to write or enjoy refined classical music and organizing your self-respect.

Days when you are in a flesh emotional mood are good days to organize your emotional feelings and to relax in flesh-colored environments.

Days when you are in a flesh sexual mood are good days for building sexual confidence by acknowledging that you can put it all together sexually.

Violet

Days when you are in a violet spiritual mood are good days for feeling cheerful about being a dedicated and idealistic type person; also good for being psychically open and imaginative, and for writing.

Days when you are in a violet mental mood are good days for using your psychic mental powers and for planning dignified and dedicated activities.

Days when you are in a violet vocal mood are good days for vocalizing the regality and stature of your voice and sending telepathic messages.

Days when you are in a violet physical mood are good days for starting dedicated physical exercise.

Days when you are in a violet control mood are good days to concentrate on being regal and dedicated in a controlled manner; also for studying and reading information on good posture and image projection.

Days when you are in a violet emotional mood are good days to feel and project your regal and dedicated emotions to others and yourself; also for tuning in to your emotional intuitiveness.

Days when you are in a violet sexual mood are good days to express your dedicated and powerful sexual commitments to your loved one and enjoying sex in violet colored environments.

Red

Days when you are in a red spiritual mood will be good days to be open minded about forgiveness, compassion, feeling youthful and happy and imaginative and truthful about love-making, and listening to romantic music to uplift your spirit.

Days when you are in a red mental mood will be good days for being practical in analyzing your romantic situation and analyzing anything of a physical nature, and being truthful.

Days when you are in a red vocal mood will be good days to let your romantic and truthful feelings flow and vibrate through your vocal center.

Days when you are in a red physical mood will be good days for enjoying your physical life forces and for expressing romance from your heart.

Days when you are in a red control mood will be good days to express your romantic feelings with a sense of dignity, control and self-respect.

Days when you are in a red emotional mood will be good days to express your romantic mood in an emotional way and relaxing in a red romantic setting.

Days when you are in a red sexual mood are good days to enjoy your romantic sexual impulses with your loved one, in red romantic environments.

Orange

Days when you are in a orange spiritual mood are good days to be imaginative and open to creative ideas in any field; also good for feeling youthful and wholesome about being kind and warm towards others and yourself.

Days when you are in a orange mental mood are good days for analyzing creative ideas in a practical way and also for realizing that being warm and kind to others and yourself has its practical benefits also.

Days when you are in a orange vocal mood are good days to be creative with your voice and practice deep, warm, resonant exercises with your vocal center.

Days when you are in a orange physical mood are good days to be creative physically—pottery, painting, woodcarving, sculpturing, and days for giving nice, warm, kind hugs to people you love.

Days when you are in a orange control mood are good days for feeling regal and dignified about being a kind, creative, and warm person, and for taking on creative tasks that require an extra degree of control and refinement.

Days when you are in a orange emotional mood are good days to be kind and warm and emotionally creative; these are very good days to "communicate" emotionally with others.

Days when you are in a orange sexual mood are good days to show your loved one both your warm and kind sexuality and your "dynamic versatility" and creative, sexual traits and enjoy sex in an orange environment.

Yellow

Days when you are in a yellow spiritual mood are good days for feeling very optimistic and cheerful, a good day to be open about intellectual ideas and a good day to praise God for all you have.

Days when you are in a yellow mental mood are good days to analyze any intellectual or scientific theories you have.

Days when you are in a yellow vocal mood are good days for vocalizing any cheerful feelings you have through your vocal center.

Days when you are in a yellow physical mood are good days to let your body feel youthful and light and cheerful.

Days when you are in a yellow control mood are good days to show your optimism and intellect in a regal manner.

Days when you are in a yellow emotional mood are excellent days for laughing cheerfully and sharing your cheerful emotions.

Days when you are in a yellow sexual mood are good days for sharing the cheerful and optimistic side of sex, and using your intellectual knowledge of sexual matters, and enjoying sex in yellow colored environments.

Green

Days when you are in a green spiritual mood are good days to take a trip to wherever there are a lot of trees or greenery for a very spiritual uplifting feeling, and also good for balancing your spiritual thoughts.

Days when you are in a green mental mood are good days to let your mind be balanced and peaceful in a practical way, and analyzing methods of balancing structures, etc.

Days when you are in a green vocal mood are good days for balancing through your voice.

Days when you are in a green physical mood are good days to practice walking for "fashion turns" if you want to be a model. Also, for taking good physical exercise walks around green trees, etc.

Days when you are in a green control mood are good days to express your balanced, controlled nature in a very regal and dignified way.

Days when you are in a green emotional mood are excellent days for sitting under green trees or walking in the forest to relax and balance your emotions.

Days when you are in a green sexual mood are good days to balance your sexual feelings and to enjoy sex in a green environment.

Blue

Days when you are in a blue spiritual mood are good days to take advantage of having faith in all things working out, a very good day to throw out all the worries; also good days to be spiritual and soulful; a good day to let your imagination search the wide open meditative blue.

Day when you are in a blue mental mood are good days to be soulful in a practical way and for using your imaginative, analytical abilities, and for being dutiful in a practical way.

Days when you are in a blue vocal mood are good days to practice or enjoy soulful songs or sounds.

Days when you are in a blue physical mood are good days for feeling physically spirited and flowing soulfully.

Days when you are in a blue control mood are good days for showing your faith in a controlled manner.

Days when you are in a blue emotional mood are good days for being emotionally soulful and laughing soulfully and relaxing around blue waters, blue skies, etc.

Days when you are in a blue sexual mood are good days to enjoy and show your open soulful sexual traits with your love one and enjoy sex around blue environments.

White-Gray-Black

Use the positive traits that I mentioned in the white, gray and black chapter; when you are in any of these color center moods.

10

How We Interact with Other Color Chemistry Types

10

How We Interact with Other Color Chemistry Types

The life-long color traits that affect our seven energy centers have very strong affects on how we interact with others. There are three types of chemistry relationships - opposites, similarities, and differential. Here are the ways these types interact.

Opposites

Yellow - Violet

Blue - Orange

Green - Red

Flesh is harmonious with all other colors since it contains all the colors.

Let's use the spiritual center. For example: (G)ina and (R)obert will be spiritual opposites. The "G" in Gina's name vibrates to the blue spectrum, whereas the "R" in Robert vibrates to the orange spectrum. If one looks at a color wheel they will see that these two are opposite each other on this wheel. These two will have an abundance spiritually of what the other doesn't have. It's like, if two people were making bread, and the two main ingredients in making bread were flour and water, and one person had all the flour, and one had all the water, well, then they need each others ingredients. Opposites are so different that they humor and amaze one another. Spiritual opposites will humor one another spiritually. Emotional opposites will humor each other emotionally. Sexual opposites will humor each other sexually, and so on with all the center opposites. Remember, laughter breaks up hard feelings as I stated earlier, and during the course of any long relationship, there's going to be some bad feelings now and then. If these bad feelings are not broken down they will just get worse. So, if you get too worked up, let your opposite humor, defuse and balance you! Opposites are so different they actually find the other interesting and seldom boring. I have observed that when opposites first meet, they seem very foreign to one another because of these great differences. But don't let this recoil you. Give it time, and you will usually find what wonderfully stimulating feelings these relationships can develop. Opposites are like magnets. They don't attract until they're put closer together. But once they bond, they're hard to take apart. I will also assume not all opposites will get along, because of different maturity levels. This is one of the possible defects in these situations.

If you don't have any center - color opposites between you and your mate, you could consider making up fun little nicknames for each other which start with opposite letters. For example: (S)ugar and (P)umpkin. (S) to yellow and (P) to violet.

The key to successful opposite relationships are: helping one another through humor, balancing, and giving advice to one another what knowledge the other lacks. Opposite relationships can be very clean, faithful, wholesome, happy, and fun relationships in whatever center your opposites are or you choose them to be located: spiritual, mental, vocal, physical, control, emotional, or sexual.

Similarities

Those persons with the same color letters in their same centers will stimulate each other in those centers. They have the same color traits. These similarities can have very stimulating and relaxing times together because of these double strong agreement qualities. They must also be aware of the tendency to over stimulate or overdo in these same traits and learn to use a certain amount of control if they tend to be too stimulating.

Example: (D)on and (D)ebbie or Sa(m) and Pa(m)

The key to successful similarity couples are: helping one another by way of stimulating through agreeance and exhilaration in combination with control and caution.

Differential Color Harmonies

This will be any color that isn't your opposite or stimulating similarities. These relationships will be different. They can be very warm, mature, and educational for each other. These people can get along fine, because they can offer different points of view, and share different viewpoints. But, they must recognize that they are different, and must act mature in letting each other be themself. They must just realize that they are different and concentrate on the "maturity" of each other's traits. (Example: (R)obert and (S)andy or Al-(f)red and Sal-(l)y.) Remember maturity, along with other factors such as environmental experiences, upbringing, and social status will play a part on how good or bad these situations can be. The key to successful differential viewpoints is by helping one another to express their different points of view in a mature, kind, respectful, and considerate manner.

Other relationships (such as with friends, co-workers, and superiors) will hold to these general rules. But when one knows where others lie in their basic traits, be it spiritual, physical, emotional, etc., then one can better understand these people and have a better chance to improve their relationship.

11
The 'Will', the 'Way'
and the 'Habit'

11
The 'Will', the 'Way' and the 'Habit'

The Three Ways to Cultivate your Talents!

The three basic ways to succeed at cultivating your talents are (1) you must have the will to succeed and continue to remind yourself; some choose to, others don't . . .(2) you have to know the way— you've heard the saying "Where there is a will, there is a way!"— which can be accomplished by sitting down and getting in touch with your spiritual center (I have explained that is your openminded creative imagination center, your faith center). Before you can succeed, you have to have faith that you can succeed, you have to visualize yourself succeeding. Then you must get in touch with your mental center (I have explained that is your practical- organization center, your practical problem solver center). In a very practical and organized way, list all your known talents and assets and use the ROLLIET LETTER COLOR SYSTEM to find your hidden natural talents which were either undiscovered or uncultivated, and go down the list. Decide which one (or ones) you wish or need to cultivate or have the best chance of cultivating successfully. After making your decisions, figure out (again in a practical way) the best ways to go about achieving your goals. Lastly, to succeed, the third step is *habit*. I can't emphasize the importance of this word enough.

If you stop to think about it, we start to learn habits while in our mother's womb. Through birth, childhood and continuing through our lifetime, we learn the habits of eating, sleeping, walking, enjoying, fearing, loving, thinking etc.

Once we learn these habits, it becomes harder to change them. Do you think a person who smokes all their life finds it hard to quit this habit?—YES! You better believe it! Do you think a left— handed person can become right-handed overnight?—HARDLY NOT! Do you believe a professional musician becomes a professional without the habit of practice and learning and cultivating this talent? Does a professional basketball player become a pro by playing basketball a few times in a lifetime? — NO way! He takes his natural talent and exposes these talents to many days and many years of habitually playing, dribbling, and shooting. Do you think that alot of people in our society (who focus on money and material gains), have forgotten or neglected the cultivation of their spiritual, physical, or emotional centers? — YES, I think so!

Now the question is, "What bad habits have you started? How do you change these self-defeating habits that you would like to break?"

Well, I have a saying that goes like this, "To break an *old bad habit*, you must replace it with a *new good habit*". Begin practicing whatever center traits you wish to cultivate and project. Remember don't give up!

Look for my next book in the near future, which will provide detailed information on CREATING ANY OF the 7 IMAGES (creative, intellectual, vocal, dramatic, corporate, romantic, and sensual), and will also explore the career fields that are aligned to these different character types.

12
Making and
Organizing Money

12
Making and
Organizing Money

Now that we have established ways of finding and cultivating your talents, the next step is the application of those talents for financial gain. As I have mentioned previously, making money and managing it is basically a mental center function. For those that want and need to make and manage money wisely, I strongly suggest cultivating this center! (Both their life-long mental traits and their daily mental color traits as discussed in Chapter 9).

First you must apply your talents to the field in which they pertain. If someone has cultivated very cheerful spiritually mature traits, then they should work in a career field that will allow expression and capitalization of this talent, where it would be appreciated and rewarded. If a person has cultivated one's physical or control center traits, then one should apply these talents to a related field. Yes, this is common simple "practical" sense, and I will continue to stress this basic philosophy. If a person is earning good wages, but spends too much on fancy cars or other luxury items and can't save money, what is the simple logical practical solution to save money? Yes, refrain from buying those extras! What if a person works in a low paying job or company? That person needs to change jobs or employer. However, before one does this they must sit down and devise a step-by-step practical plan.

Practical, practical, practical, that's the message. It's the most important word in making money. I have seen so many new businesses fail, because the people operating them are using their spiritual center traits or their control traits or emotional center traits in an unpractical manner. Don't get me wrong, these traits are all necessary to a certain degree when operating a business. You need that good old "Rah! Rah! Let's go!" spirit. You need that new regal suit for that "power image" in some cases to project self control and comand financial respect. You also need to be emotionally involved in your profession to a certain extent. But you ask any successful business person, and they will agree the most important factor in getting a company to make money is "common practical sense". If you were to ask these same successful people their opinion about any particular business' chance of succeeding, you would continually hear common practical questions such as: Is there a market for it? Are there others out there that have control of that market? Does it cost more to make and market your product than what you could sell it for? Is there enough parking space around your business? Is there enough population in the area in which you plan to locate? Is there enough foot traffic? Can you handle the stresses that are involved? Do you have enough money to start up? Is this something that you just want to do, or do you think you can really make money from it? Is there a need for it? Can you be competitive? Have you asked others their opinions?

These are all questions that are basically asking you, "have you sat down in a "practical" manner, and exercised your mental center traits, to determine if your product or service has a 'practical chance of success'? Long shots do come in sometimes, but nine out of ten successes are won on "practicality". Such old sayings as "Don't jump into it just on a whim;" "Don't get impulsive;" "Check it out first" are all precautions meant to stimulate one's "practical mental center".

So, sit down. Now, organize yourself, taking into account all factors, and go out and make money and manage it in a practical way. You can and should use your mental center for making other important decisions such as love-mates, health, self-control and matters that need well-grounded common sense judgement.

13
Lifestyles and Colors

13
Lifestyles and Colors

We all have a certain lifestyle which requires appropriate wardrobe styles and colors. For example, a business person that works in a conservative business field must adhere to the appropriate clothing styles and colors to be regarded with respect. However, one can follow these certain rules but still utilize one's individual color traits in accessories such as ties, shirts, pins, etc. The general rule of styles and colors are to dress basically as your peers and associates.

Businessmen

Businessmen should dress basically in conservative styles in either dark pin-striped blue suits or medium to dark gray suits. These are by far the most widely accepted colors in the conservative business world. Here is my reasoning for this. As I stated previously, some of the characteristics of the blue spectrum are faith, reliability, stability and sense of duty. The dark blue traits project this. Gray is the other color preferred by the conservative business world, because of its neutral emotional trait. The business world usually does not want strong emotional decision traits as part of their decision making image. They want decisions made fundamentally based on facts and not emotions.

Businesswomen

Businesswomen test best by wearing conservative suits in solid colors of medium gray and medium dark blue. Businesswomen should not wear pinstripe suits. It tested very badly in all surveys. Colors that tested well were charcoal gray, steel gray, navy, black, camel, dark brown, beige, dark maroon, dark rust. The success of these colors will differ depending on locale, etc.

In my next book, I will illustrate and discuss in detail the best styles, colors, patterns, etc. for businesswomen and other career styles.

Contemporary Fashion Industry

Those in sales positions in the contemporary fashion industry should wear contemporary styles and colors. If working towards advancement they should at times show the ability to wear conservative suits to allow senior management to see their executive potential and the ability to project that image. If a person wears *only* youthful or trendy contemporary clothes upper executives will perceive this person only in this manner, just as some actors or actresses get type cast. When one desires to move up the ladder, I suggest dressing contemporary at times, and also dressing conservatively at other times to indicate a desire for upper mobility, and doing so appropriately. Also express your goals and desires directly to management – they love to hear it.

When attending a sporting event, wear casual sportswear. If you are attending a casual event, dress casually. If you are attending a black tie event, wear black tie. If you are going to the mountains, wear the type of clothing you'll need for the occasion. Style and color dressing is just basic common sense. There are exceptions to this where we all need some advice and should seek it. Generally, it is best to observe how others "in the know" dress.

Lines, Patterns and Textures

I would briefly like to discuss lines, patterns, and textures because as we know, the clothes that we wear not only come in colors, but also in these different lines, patterns, and textures. Let me start with pinstriped straight lines, especially those that are used in business suits and shirts. If we look and analyze these straight lines, we will see that they have no deviations in them. They are conforming, straight and to the point. In other words, "no-nonsense", very strict, ridged, predictable, in order, and in sequence. They also create tallness and stature. These are the general traits expected of business men.

Let us now look at solid suits, which are also acceptable in business suits for men, but more acceptable for business women. Solid suits have a wider, more open look and effect. They reflect the traits of spaciousness, openness, thoughtfulness, and analysis.

Why do business women test higher, wearing solid suits versus pinstriped suits? At this point, I can only say that it is related to the different masculine and feminine roles that society has placed on men and women! Probably, men have emotional walls built around them, whereas women are supposed to be emotionally open.

Patterns hold basically to the same rules in ties and scarfs. If the pattern is orderly, in a repetitive, small, and conservative manner, it will be acceptable for business.

Texture, luster and sheen hold basically to the rules of amount and order. They can be used in ties and scarfs, but hardly ever in larger amounts for business persons! Entertainers, yes! Business persons, no!

So I will say again observe those who are "in the know" and dress in the image that reflects your position or expected image in your field!

Strong and Weak Features and Traits

We all have strong and weak physical features and personality traits. I am often asked "What colors or patterns will make me look taller or thinner?" "How can I look heavier or younger of more energetic and vibrant?" The list goes on. Some of these questions are answered in the daily color chapter, but here are some general rules of affects of colors, patterns, textures, and sheens:

Patterns and Textures

Vertical pinstripe lines will make you appear:
1. taller
2. thinner
3. authoritative
4. businesslike (no-nonsense)
5. non deviating (rigid)
6. decisive
7. regal

Flower prints, loose or lively prints will make you appear:
1. friendlier
2. carefree
3. happier
4. romantic
5. "on vacation" (doesn't that sound nice)

Rough thick textures will make you appear:
1. masculine
2. physical
3. earthier
4. aggressive

Soft and thin fabrics will make you appear:
1. feminine
2. romantic
3. relaxed
4. refined

Colors and Sheens

Light colors will make you appear:
1. lighter
2. wider (broader)
3. energetic (active)
4. cheerful and approachable
5. spiritual

Medium colors will make you appear:
1. neutral (neither aggressive nor timid)
2. factual
3. contemplative
4. balanced

Darker colors will make you appear:
1. heavier
2. shorter
3. consuming (in listening)
4. earthier
5. open (but in a serious manner)

Shiny or high-luster colors will make you appear:
1. sexy and seductive
2. dramatic (flamboyant)
3. energetic (dynamic)
4. glamorous

Flat textures will make you appear:
1. conservative
2. practical
3. relaxed

You should also turn what you or others consider weak features into positive ones. If you happen to be 4 ft. 8 in. and want to be 6 ft. well this just isn't practical so just project and imagine what a dynamic and energetic and mature person is inside that 4 ft. 8 in. frame! and let others know you're bigger and much more important than most think! If you happen to be 6 ft. 8 in. and would like to be 5 ft. 8 in. well this again isn't practical, so just view and project yourself as being very authoritative and of a commanding stature that this tallness suggests. Make the best of what you possess and what you can't change don't concentrate on it, because it will have a negative effect on you (accentuate the positive and eliminate the negative).

14
Interior Decorators

14
Interior Decorators

How can an interior decorator create a relaxed elegant room environment for a customer, without knowing that person's life- long emotional colors? How can they create a regal-formal-power environment if they don't know that customer's life-long Control Center colors? How can a decorator create a sexually stimulating environment for a person, if they don't know that person's sexual center colors? It would be advantageous for interior decorators and designers to learn the Rolliet Color System so that they would be able to know how each color affects each individual for a greater percentage of the time.

For example: Jane Dobb

This person is a red-orange spiritual. These are the primary colors I would advise for a clean, spirited, fresh room.

This person is a double-flesh mental. I would advise this color for a study or a practical, mental, organizational space.

This person is a blue-violet sexual. I would advise these colors to achieve a sexual effect.

This person is a yellow-green emotional person. I would advise these colors for a relaxed romantic effect. (The "e" in her first name is silent).

15

Fashion, Cosmetic and Jewelry Industries

15
Fashion, Cosmetic and
Jewelry Industries

Fashion Industry

I've had the personal experience of being told by fashion salespersons, that many stores were 'turned off' by certain color analysts because they limit their potential customers to buying just certain seasonal colors, while the store would like customers to buy during all seasons, in all colors. In addition, the stores do not want their sales to have any limiting factors involved. The Rolliet Color System Theory serves both the customers' needs and preferences, and stimulates buying to satisfy the store's preferences. It also gives the store a greater ability to help the customer's true needs. Once a person finds out their power colors, they want to buy garments in those colors. Once a person finds out their, or their love-mates sexual colors, they want to buy garments in those colors. Once a person finds out their spiritual-youthful colors, they want to buy garments in those colors, and so on. Not only does the Rolliet System advise persons to purchase garments in their life-long colors for life-long situations, but stresses the importance of a wardrobe with a full-range of colors to meet their important daily color needs.

Cosmetic Industry

My next book will be directed in part towards the cosmetic industry and the use of cosmetics. At this time, I must admit that my application of the Rolliet Color Theory to the use of make-up and other cosmetics is in its first stages. Therefore, I will withhold from making any firm statements, except to say that the Rolliet Color Systems should hold true to the use of cosmetics. Look for future information or feel free to contact me in the near future regarding this application.

Jewelry Industry

I know of no better industries than the fashion and jewelry industries, that I can immediately and in such a convincing manner, show the visual physical proof, that the Rolliet Color System is credible and effective. If we stop to think about it, colored, precious or even glass colored jewelry has the ability to reflect, illuminate, and sparkle the colors of the spectrum better than any other earthy material substance. I strongly suggest that the jewelry industries use the Rolliet Color System if they wish to get the maximum effect of showing off their wares. For example, a person that is in a spiritual red mood could not project any more youthful and spirited, than by wearing that red color and wearing sparkling red jewelry. A blue-control mood person could not look anymore regal-royal and in control and powerful than by wearing any color, other than blue, with wearing sparkling blue jewelry! This belief holds true for all of the other center colors!

16
Colors in Business Advertising

16
Colors in
Business Advertising

I ask all businesses, "how can an actor or actress project or relay their message if they don't get their feelings in touch with that mood message which they wish to project"? "How can a race car driver expect to win if he doesn't use the best tires, the best fuel, or get the best out of his pit crew?" "How can a professional sports organization get the most out if its players if it doesn't utilize them properly or in the right positions?" "What if a football team used its' quarterback as a tackle or nose guard, or its' tackle in the quarterback position?" "What if a baseball team used its' power hitter in the 9th batting position and its' weakest hitter in the cleanup spot?"

The answer to those questions are quite simple. They're just not going to get the MAXIMUM BENEFIT out of those players and positions! Now, I ask all businesses that advertise their logo—(business cards, signs, packages, and multi-media advertisements)—how do you expect to get the maximum effect from your advertisement, if you don't use the correct colors in the advertisement?

For example — if a company is promoting a romantic product — use pink-tinted colors as the dominant colors in the packaging of this product or message. If a company is trying to project a intellectual image, I would advise the colors in the yellow spectrum as the dominant colors.

If a company wanted to project its own image of being poised, balanced, and in control, I would advise the green spectrum. I strongly advise all businesses to learn the spiritual, physical and emotional traits of the colors and the spiritual, emotional and physical color traits of their customers if they want to give their customers the best service possible and reap the best possible results from their advertisements.

Let me give some examples of common words used in commercials for hair products. The traits they refer to most often in their advertisements to promote hair products match the traits found in our seven centers. Shiny, youthful, clean, wholesome, happy, fun – aren't these spiritual center traits? Silky, suave, smooth, soft – aren't these sexual and emotional center traits? I would advise using the models daily colors in the clothes and jewelry she wears, and also in background colors to achieve these mood images to support and accentuate around her hair!

When a company hires a model to represent their product or company image, would it not be more advantageous to pick a person that has cultivated the center-color character traits that are in tune with this product or message? I would strongly advise all companies using models or spokepersons to ask your advertising or modeling agency if they use the Rolliet Color System with their models? If they say no, I would advise that you recommend it for best results!

17
Entertainment Industry

17
Entertainment Industry

Again, I ask the same basic questions: How can an actor playing a very dramatic role look the most dramatic, if he doesn't also wear his most dramatic color? How can an actress who is playing a youthful and spirited role look and project that image, if she doesn't wear her spiritual color? How can a beauty queen look and project her sexiest or most regal image if she doesn't tune into those colors? How can a dance company that is dancing a romantic number project this, if they are not garbed in a romantic color? How can a singer best project an emotional mood, if they don't wear their emotional color when performing that emotional song? How can a television or movie company expect their actors and actresses to play a sad part wearing a cheerful yellow colored costume and expect to get the most dramatic effect out of that particular scene?

As for character actors, if I were casting for a movie and I needed a person to play a very regal-royal part in a dramatic manner, I would look for a person with violet dramatic letter traits because this would be a natural part for this type person. If I were looking for a person to play a very warm, kind, emotionally creative part, I would look for an orange emotional person. Again, this type person would be a natural for the part. Maximum benefit can be achieved by using the Rolliet Color System.

18

Educational Institutions and Employers

18
Educational Institutions and Employers

How can schools help students to cultivate their natural talents if they don't know what they are? How can they help a student who is having emotional problems relax emotionally if they don't know that student's natural emotional relaxing traits? How can they help a student who is depressed to become cheerful if they don't know their spiritual center traits?

Some of the most important aspects of life are to "LEARN, GROW, MATURE and CULTIVATE" one's natural talents and abilities, so that a person can achieve feelings of self-worth and a sense of belonging, and contributing to the betterment of society. How many times have we made statements such as "I should have cultivated my talents a lot more?" How many of us have realized certain talents that we had, but waited too long to cultivate them?

There are so many people who have wonderful potential that just lie dormant all their lives – it's a shame. Educational institutions could do well by using the ROLLIET COLOR THEORY to help students discover their natural talents. Employers in all fields could use the system to tap into their employees talents and bring out the BEST in them. A company may have a very creative employee, but unless they know this, the person who has these talents may never be utilized.

19
Drugs versus Colors

19
Drugs versus Colors

Drugs have very strong affects on us. The main reason is because they are usually very concentrated in whatever chemical substance they possess. Have you ever taken one small pill (not even 1/4 of an inch in diameter), and then later wondered how could something so small have such a powerful effect on a large physical body? Well, the answer basically lies partially on the concentration, and also on the specific small portion of the brain that this drug affects. The brain either quits sending out electrical impulses or releases large or smaller quantities of hormones or chemicals which either increases or decreases different body organ functions (spiritual, mental, vocal, physical, control, emotional, or sexual). I will use this opportunity to again support my belief that electromagnetic color wavelength impulses that travel through our ears to our brain, which effects our seven centers in a similar way as drugs, but much more subtly.

Drugs have very strong side effects. Sound and visual color vibrations side effects? Only research and time will tell. What if concentration of color vision and color audio impulses are increased and exalted to very acute levels ? I could tell you of a first hand experience I had with a color experiment that I performed on myself, which had a very strong effect on me, but I will refrain from doing this. I strongly advise against anyone from doing any uncontrolled experiments of this nature, because of possible harmful effects.

Homeopathic doctors talk about a person's dynamic force that possibly controls our immune system and has the ability to help heal us and protect us. When this dynamic force is weakened, we can become susceptible to disease and sickness. Can this dynamic force be our spiritual center-color vibration force traits, or our physical center color force, or a balance in all of our center color forces? This could be an interesting field of study for those involved in homeopathic medicine research.

"The great importance of color lies in the fact that it can influence all the different aspects of man-physical, emotional, mental and spiritual, and so help to produce that harmony which itself implies perfect health".

"The human body is composed of cells. The basis of life is the atom. Within the atom are vibrating particles-negatively charged electrons circling around positively charged protons. Beyond this, color therapy postulates a rhythmic order of vibrations of several degrees, the lowest and coarsest being the physical, then the emotional, and then the mental. Health is harmony and disease is discord. Illness may arise in the physical, emotional, or mental sphere".

"Is it too visionary to imagine a time when diseases will be classified by their wavelength and the counteracting of them become a mathematical certainty"? –J. Dodson Hessey

20
Colors and the Deaf and Blind

20

Colors and the Deaf and Blind

Let me start this chapter by asking a question, which surprisingly I have not been asked by anyone, other than myself. If hearing your name effects your chemistry traits in your seven centers, what about those that are deaf? How are their basic life- long color traits determined? Well, let me first say that my answer at this time is purely conjecture.

First, remember color wavelengths are very subtle and invisible, so they could well pass through the inner ear and still have a unconscious effect.

Second, we do not get all of our color vibrations via our hearing sense. We have over two million cones and rods in our eyes that take in light and colors. These are then sent to our brains. So for deaf people I presume that their general life-long color associations would be determined by visually learned experiences. For example, certain home environments could play key roles such as the colored room in which a person was used to relaxing, could become this person's relax-emotion color, or a certain color room in which one played when very young could become this person's dramatic physical color, and so on, along with the rest of the center-colors. Let me also add that we eat foods that are different colors, and our skin absorbs light and colors. We also breathe in light and colors, and we read certain written color associations from others such as "Green with envy," "I was in a fit of purple rage," "I was so angry I could see red", "Pretty in pink," possibly the deaf operate primarily off of their daily color mood traits vibrations. What about those that are both deaf and blind, do they have any color associations? Let me conclude by relaying a very interesting discovery by a German scientist, Dr Anschutz, some years ago, as quoted by Corinne Heline in her book "Healing and Regeneration Through Color."

Dr. Anschutz has issued numerous pamphlets and books on his researches. He has shown that a large number of persons connect each musical note with a tint, more or less precisely. More rarely they perceive a world of color when they hear music. He reports as a specifically interesting case of "color hearing" that of an organist, Dorken, blind from the age of thirteen years.

This man, despite his blindness, has retained a vivid memory of colors. Each note of the scale means for him a very definite tint. Each human voice produces a luminous vision-pleasant or otherwise: each odor has its photism, every vivid sensation such as muscular fatigue, toothache, even a bath, produces one. Sneezing brings it on. This sensitiveness would not seem to be a manifestation of disease.

Several professors of philosophy have aided him by making inquiries in their classes. The material thus gathered proved that synesthesia or "color hearing" is not so rare as has been thought and not necessarily abnormal. – Corinne Heline

Heline adds "this work of Dr. Anschutz is but a forerunner of many groups which will be organized to study the mysteries of color and music and to learn to use a synthesis of color and tone for healing the 'physical ills' of man, and also to 'accentuate and accelerate' his 'moral and spiritual development'."

21
General Rules and Uses of Colors and Centers

21
General Rules and Uses
of Colors and Centers

I have one basic piece of advice on the use of your colors and centers and their traits and that is as God has told us - use everything in moderation. Do not abuse your powers for selfish gains or excessive goals. One needs to balance a center in relation to its other centers. Our centers are like gears in a clock; they are interdependent. If one is off, it tends to throw off the whole clock. So if you need to relax, then put the emphasis on your relaxing emotional center colors. If one needs to make practical, intelligent decisions, then work on your intellectual center. Good luck and God bless!

General Signs of Excess Use of Centers

Spiritual - Feeling of carrying the world's problems on your shoulders, too open, spread too thin, too gullible, too subservient.

Mental - Feeling of confusion, scattered mind, too much analyzing, tired or chattering mind, insomnia.

Vocal - Hoarse voice, lost voice.

Physical - prone to injury, broken bones, sprained ankles and injuries in general, too aggressive, too dramatic.

Control - Too snobbish, too power hungry, petty criticisms.

Emotional - Emotional breakdown, excessive crying, upset stomach, stomach problems, sleeping problems.

Sexual - Sexual perversion, sexual malfunctions and diseases.

General Signs of Too Little Use of Centers

Spiritual - No spiritual beliefs, narrow mindedness, lack of spirit, feeling old, unimaginative, too earthy, violent philosophies.

Mental - Dumbfounded, scattered, inability to be logical, analytical, or practical.

Vocal - Too soft or inaudible voice, not being able to express self in words, poor auditory memory.

Physical - Out of shape, poor muscle tone, etc.

Control - Lack of control, impulsive eating or buying, excessive compulsive habits, lack of power and dignity (self respect).

Emotional - Too impersonal, inability to communicate emotionally with others.

Sexual - Sexual fridigity, lack of interest, and sexual dysfunctions.

22
Naming
Your Children

22
Naming
Your Children

You can help to determine your children's traits by the names you pick or if you have already decided, you will know what their natural traits may be. You can slowly start to expose them to those fields or careers. Remember not to force them into what you want them to be, let them decide. Simply provide exposure and allow them access to their natural talents. They should become attached to at least one of them, and they'll probably excel in one of those fields with proper guidance. You'll also know the negative sides of their center colors and can help to guide them away from any negative behavior.

For example: Randy Baker is a:

Orange and violet spiritual person

Double flesh mental person

Blue and orange vocal person

Blue and flesh control person

Double orange physical person

Red and green emotional person

Now you would apply these color traits to those centers both positively and negatively, to better know the natural traits of this person. For example, this person is a double orange physical person as well as being an orange spiritual person, (which is his imaginative and enthusiasm center). The creative field in which this person would probably excel would be a physical creative field, (such as pottery, painting, wood carving) and certain sports. This person is also a double flesh mental person (the practical organizing color), so this person would more than likely be a excellent organizer and money manager. But remember, a person can apply their traits to any number of different fields.

On the negative side, this person is a double orange physical person, and as I stated in the orange color chapter, when an orange physical person's spirit turns bad, he may have a very strong tendency to become physically destructive, rather than the positive traits of creativeness, kindness, and constructiveness. Therefore, this person should be made aware of this tendency beforehand, to guard against the negative action.

You can also add or change letters in their names to improve or acquire the traits you wish. For example: if your child is already involved in learning musical skills, you can change or add any of the flesh letters (A, H, O, V) to their names, especially the first letter in their name to give them increased musical imagination; for example: from (Gin) to (V)irgini(a). If you have a son whose name is Richie and he is involved in creative arts, you could add some physical creative traits to his name by changing it from (R)ichie to (R)ic(k)y. Then he would have both creative spiritual imagination first letter trait and the physical creative letter trait in his name.

Bibliography

Bibliography

Abbeville Press, Inc., NY - Women Artist 1988.

Birren Faber, Color & Human Response, Van Nostrand Co., NY, 1978.

Birren, Faber, Color Psychology and Color Therapy, Citadel Press, Secaucus, NJ, 1978.

Birren, Faber, Color in Your World, Collier Books, New York, NY, 1978.

Berkeley Holistic Health Center, The New Holistic Health Handbook, The Stephen Greene Press, Lexington, MA, 1985

Dixie Hall, The Artists, Walter T. Foster Art Books, Tustin, CA.

Ladybird Books LTD, "Light" Toughborough Teicestershire, England.

Hunt, Roland T., "The Eighth Key to Color", J.N. Fowler & Co., LTD, London, England, 1965.

Heline, Corinne, Healing and Regeneration Through Color, New Age Press, Inc., La Canda, CA, 1976.

Molloy, John T., Dress for Success, Warner Books, NY, 1975.

Molloy, John T., The Womans Dress for Success Book, Warner Books, NY, 1977.

Do It Yourself Life-Long Color Chart

W A R D R O B E   I M A G E S

CENTER	COLOR	COLOR	COLOR	IMAGE	IMAGE	IMAGE	IMAGE
SPIRITUAL							
MENTAL							
VOCAL							
PHYSICAL							
CONTROL							
EMOTIONAL							
SEXUAL							

H O M E   D E C O R – M O O D   E N V I R O N M E N T S

CENTER	COLOR	COLOR	COLOR	ROOM	ROOM	ROOM	ROOM
SPIRITUAL							
MENTAL							
VOCAL							
PHYSICAL							
CONTROL							
EMOTIONAL							
SEXUAL							

C A R E E R   A L T E R N A T I V E S

CENTER	COLOR	COLOR	COLOR	CAREER	CAREER	CAREER	CAREER
SPIRITUAL							
MENTAL							
VOCAL							
PHYSICAL							
CONTROL							
EMOTIONAL							
SEXUAL							

Do It Yourself Life-Long Color Chart

SAMPLE NAME: SANDY LARKON

WARDROBE IMAGES							
CENTER	COLOR	COLOR	COLOR	IMAGE	IMAGE	IMAGE	IMAGE
SPIRITUAL	yellow	yellow		youthful	creative	cheerful	
MENTAL	flesh	flesh		practical	logical		
VOCAL	blue	orange		fluent			
PHYSICAL	orange	orange		dramatic	assertive	physical	
CONTROL	blue	orange		corporate	refined	negal	formal
EMOTIONAL	red	violet	green	romantic	relaxed	feminine	
SEXUAL	orange	blue		Sexy	earthy		

HOME DECOR – MOOD ENVIRONMENTS							
CENTER	COLOR	COLOR	COLOR	ROOM	ROOM	ROOM	ROOM
SPIRITUAL	yellow	yellow		Kitchen	Rec.R.		
MENTAL	flesh	flesh		office	study	music	
VOCAL	blue	orange		music			
PHYSICAL	orange	orange		art studio	exercise		
CONTROL	blue	orange		dining	office		
EMOTIONAL	red	violet	green	bedroom	living	Patio	
SEXUAL	orange	blue		bedroom			

CAREER ALTERNATIVES							
CENTER	COLOR	COLOR	COLOR	CAREER	CAREER	CAREER	CAREER
SPIRITUAL	yellow	yellow		Scientist	teacher		
MENTAL	flesh	flesh		finance	composer	manager	
VOCAL	blue	orange		opera			
PHYSICAL	orange	orange		potter	artist		
CONTROL	blue	orange		banker			
EMOTIONAL	red	violet	green	poet	ecologist		
SEXUAL	orange	blue		belly dancer			

To order another copy of
Your Name and Colors

Please send $15.95 for each book (includes tax & shipping) to:

Color Diplomats
P. O. Box 21
Crockett, CA 94525

Name: _____

Address: _____

_____

Phone: _____

- -

To order another copy of
Your Name and Colors

Please send $15.95 for each book (includes tax & shipping) to:

Color Diplomats
P. O. Box 21
Crockett, CA 94525

Name: _____

Address: _____

_____

Phone: _____